Plant pruning in pictures

Plant pruning in pictures

HOW, WHEN, AND WHERE TO PRUNE, AND WITH WHAT TOOLS

Trees—shrubs—evergreens—topiary—
espaliers—arbors—annuals—perennials—
vines—fruits—herbs—house plants—Bonsai
—kitchen gardens—grafted plants—in
transplanting

ILLUSTRATED STEP BY STEP WITH
320 PHOTOGRAPHS AND 74 LINE DRAWINGS

MONTAGUE FREE

AN AMERICAN GARDEN GUILD BOOK
DOUBLEDAY & COMPANY, INC.,
GARDEN CITY, NEW YORK

This book is affectionately dedicated to
RALPH S. BAILEY,
a former colleague.

Library of Congress Catalog Card Number 61-5021
Copyright © 1961 by Doubleday & Company, Inc.
All Rights Reserved
Printed in the United States of America

Foreword

THIS book is intended to be a companion volume to *Plant Propagation in Pictures* and likewise is primarily for the amateur.

There are some misguided folk who think that pruning is all wrong because, they say, it is unnatural. Nature herself is a great pruner. For example, in a forest, when trees grow too close together, the lowermost branches die and fall off because of the lack of light—a form of pruning. There are some trees, such as Willow, which self-prune by dropping some of their twigs. This is done by making an abscission layer similar to that which affects leaves, causing them to fall in the autumn.

I have tried to cover the pruning of various groups of plants—including trees, shrubs, house plants, vegetables, and fruits—as well as diverse techniques of pruning and training to produce espaliered, pollarded, and standard plants, topiary, and pleached allée, and to control insect pests and plant diseases, in addition to the more common forms of pruning necessary in the small garden.

I have not attempted to give individual attention to all plants. So if you do not find your particular problem in the Index, look at your shrub or tree and decide in which group it belongs. If, for example, it is early-blooming—flowers coming before the leaves—follow directions for other early bloomers.

There are many who have helped in the preparation of this book and to all of them go my thanks, especially to the following:

John Whiting, editor and publisher of *Flower Grower, The Home Garden Magazine,* for permission to use material (including some of my own) which has appeared in the magazine.

Cynthia Westcott, The Plant Doctor, who helped by her instant response to my request for permission to use the drawings of white-pine weevil, fire blight, and other pests from her book *Garden Enemies.*

James H. Beale for reading the manuscript and making valuable suggestions.

But most of all my wife deserves my thanks, here tendered, for neglecting her other activities to help me with the tedious mechanics which go into bookmaking.

Contents

Plant pruning in pictures

CHAPTER I

Some Principles of Pruning

PRUNING has been defined as removal of part of a plant to improve it. There are some who will question the desirability of any kind of pruning, and I can agree with this if it is done without knowledge of the plant and without knowing what pruning is expected to accomplish. It must be done at the right time and in the right manner. It is not a case of thinking, "This is a nice day. Let's get out and do some pruning." It is necessary to study the growth habits of the plants on which we are to operate and to know what we expect to accomplish.

Among the benefits which may accrue from pruning are the following. Faulty habits of growth can be corrected. It may be used to bring about earlier blooming. Flower and fruit size in many cases can be increased. It is an aid in controlling disease and insect pests. It makes it possible to rejuvenate old plants that are approaching senility.

Severe pruning during the time when a plant is dormant usually results in production of strong, leafy, vegetative shoots during the following growing season. Severe pruning should be avoided whenever possible because the vegetative growth induced may be so strong that no blossom buds are formed. Pruning when plants are growing may help them to produce flowering wood.

Severe pruning of the top when a plant is dormant may be disastrous in some cases because it stimulates strong shoot growth or water sprouts. These succulent shoots are attractive to aphids (presumably because their beaks are easily inserted in the soft tissue), which may carry the dreaded fire blight from a diseased tree to a healthy one. Among those that can be affected with fire blight are: Apple, Pear, Quince, and related plants such as Hawthorn, Pyracantha, Cotoneaster, and Mountain Ash. When pruning diseased plants it is advisable to disinfect the pruning shears by

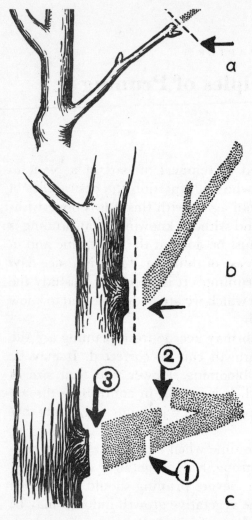

While all pruning should be done so that rapid healing will follow, there are two distinct ends which the process is designed to serve. One (a) is done in the expectation that growth will continue behind the line of cut. The second basic maneuver (b) presupposes that new growth (apart from covering bark) will not follow or be influenced by the cut. Note that the cut is made parallel to and close to the trunk. Any branches (c) too large for a shearing cut should be sawed, and any too heavy to hold should be sawed in three separate steps to avoid tearing: (1) from below until the saw binds; (2) from above, farther out, until the limb cracks; (3) then the remaining stub sawed close to the trunk.

dipping them in Formalin or alcohol before each cut; otherwise you may be spreading the disease.

Plants which bloom on old wood cannot be pruned during the time they are dormant without removing potential flowers. This does not mean that it never should be done, although in general it is better to wait until the flowers have faded before doing any cutting.

Those which bloom on shoots made during the current season (*Buddleia davidi, Vitex,* Hybrid Tea, Hybrid Perpetual Roses, and others) can be cut back severely before growth starts in the spring.

Pruning to promote growth or regulate form. Left above, dormant (pre-spring) pruning encourages extra-vigorous growth from remaining buds as shown in gray. While dormant pruning is usually done for this purpose, a secondary result is, obviously, altered shape or form of branch structure. Summer pruning, right above, done when plant is in active growth, tends to consolidate growth, to counteract too rapid or unbalanced growth, and results in a more compact plant the ensuing year.

Pruning in relation to flowering. If flower buds are removed, left above, before they open, flowers will, of course, be sacrificed for the ensuing flowering period. This holds true for spring or fall bloomers, once buds have developed. If, however, flowering wood is removed after bloom, right above, the usual tendency is for buds to develop for flowers, shown in gray, during following blooming season.

Root pruning is practiced to promote a more compact root system. In the case of trees it greatly increases the plant's ability to overcome successfully the shock of transplanting. It should be done about a year before the tree is to be moved. Root pruning may be done to promote fruitfulness. It is necessary at times to prevent trees from committing suicide, which occurs when, as sometimes happens, roots grow in such a way that they girdle the trunk and prevent free passage of water and nutrients.

Pruning can be done to correct faulty growth habits—as, for example, with the Sugar Maple, which, because its growth buds are opposite, may develop bad V-shaped crotches.

Pruning can also help control insect pests such as spruce gall aphid and white-pine shoot moth and white-pine weevil. These weevils can be fought by cutting off the infested shoots well below the injured part, and in the case of the gall aphids, the galls, which may remind you of a pineapple, should be cut off and burned before the insects leave the galls.

Pruning is not necessarily restricted to branches and roots. In some cases it is advisable to remove all faded flower clusters to prevent the formation of seeds which are a drain on the plant's energies. This is especially desirable on young plants of Lilac and Rhododendron. When the plants get older they increase in size and it becomes too much of a chore to remove all the faded clusters. Thinning fruit trees such as Apple, Pear, Peach, and Plum is advantageous. It prevents over-bearing and increases the size of the remaining fruits.

Although, ideally, pruning is done so that the natural habit of a tree or shrub is maintained, occasionally the reverse is true, as, for example, when compact hedges are required, or when individual specimens are trimmed to formal shape, and in topiary work.

When large wounds are made it is considered desirable to cover them with something to prevent the exposed wood from checking (cracking) and to keep out spores of disease-causing organisms. They should be checked at least once each year until the callus has completely covered the wound, and if necessary, the dressing should be renewed.

Tips on Techniques

Take good care of your tools. Good tools warrant good treatment. If they are really good, they will cost more and you are perhaps less likely to leave them outdoors overnight or in rain.

When using hand shears or lopping shears, do not try to cut anything that is beyond the capacity of the tool. You may be tempted to wriggle the shears, which will force the cutting blade out of alignment.

Place the cutting blade as close as possible to the branch from which the one you are cutting off originates.

Carry a sharpening hone with you so that you can keep the cutting edges sharp.

When heading back a shoot always make the cut close to the bud or lateral that is pointing in the direction that you wish the shrub or tree to grow.

Do not prune when the wood is frozen. It is brittle then and there is danger of breaking off the branches you want to keep.

Do not work when it is so cold that you are uncomfortable. You may be tempted to take short cuts and fail to give the leisurely attention that is needed when pruning.

Do not fail to unpack a shipment of trees and shrubs as soon as they are received. If the trees are bare-root ones and you are not ready to plant them right away, trim off any mangled or broken roots, heel them in, or cover them with wet Sphagnum Moss, sand, or sawdust until you are ready to plant them. It matters little what is used provided it can do the job of keeping the roots moist until they can be planted. Top growth also can be pruned at this time.

Balled and burlapped trees should be stood close together in a spot sheltered from wind and sun and watered daily. Trees have a better chance of survival if planting can proceed at once. Doubtless it is to your advantage also, since it avoids a second handling.

CHAPTER II

Tools

VARIOUS kinds of cutting tools are necessary for a would-be pruner. The simplest is a pruning knife. It is still the best tool for cutting with the least amount of injury to the plant. The one pictured is an old friend which I acquired almost sixty years ago. Its defects are: it is a dangerous tool in the hands of the unskilled or careless worker and it is slow.

Pruning knife.

Tree climber with some of his tools. Note the leather scabbard, to protect saw, the safety belt, and the carryall for small tools—chisels, hand pruner, etc.

Shears with passing-type blade with catch at the end of the handles.

Shears with passing-type blade with catch near the pivot.

Anvil-type hand pruner with catch near the pivot.

Hand pruner being used to cut out weak, spindling branches.

Shears

One-hand shears (secateurs) usually are fitted with a spring so that they open automatically and with a safety catch to keep them closed when not in use. The catch is often put at the end of the handles. This is just the right place to give the operator a blood blister, so I prefer shears with the catch near the pivot or cutting end. Two types are commonly in use, one which cuts down on an "anvil" made of comparatively soft metal or polyethylene, another in which the cutting blade passes a heavy, curved hook.

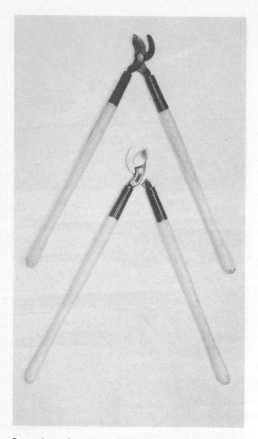

Lopping shears.

Heavy-duty lopping shears with compound lever.

Next in line are lopping shears. These are two-handled with the handles 2 to 2½ feet long. They can cut soft green wood up to 1 inch in diameter. Lopping shears of this kind are also available with a compound lever attachment which greatly magnifies the power, so that they are capable of cutting branches up to 1½ or even 2 inches. Lopping shears are useful especially when cutting out old wood from spiny subjects, such as *Rosa hugonis* and other rose species, and for pruning Blackberries, Raspberries, and Gooseberries, because they enable the operator to outwit their sometimes vicious thorns. They also are useful because the operator is given an extra 2 feet or so, which is especially valuable when cutting out overhanging tree branches.

Hedge shears.

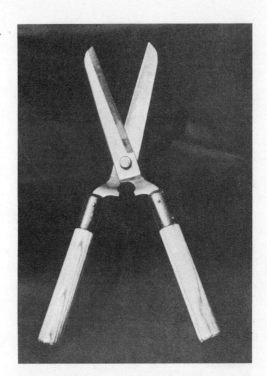

Electric hedge clippers.

Hedge shears are not pruning tools per se. Ordinarily they are to be used only for cutting hedges. Usually the over-all length of these shears is about 2 feet, but it is possible to get them with longer handles so that the over-all length is 38 inches. Anyone with 100 feet or more of hedge to be clipped should look into the possibility of using electrically operated shears. These can do the job in about one fourth the time required for manually operated hedge shears.

Pole pruner in use.

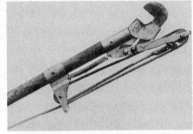

Close-up of a pole pruner with a coil spring.

Then there is the pole pruner, which is operated by a rope and pulley or by a metal rod. These usually are about 8 feet long with an extension pole of about 4 feet that can be added if necessary. In the rope-and-pulley kinds the jaws are opened by a coil spring which has to be powerful enough to do the job, and when cutting a branch the operator has to pull against the spring as well as overcome the resistance of the branch that is being cut off. There is no spring in the case of those that are operated by a metal rod. These demand a little more care on the part of the operator to avoid buckling in case the blade gets jammed, which might happen if the tool is used on extraordinarily tough wood.

Saws

The pole saw is limited in use to the cutting off of rigid branches; some branches are so wobbly that it is impossible to keep the saw in the original cuts. It is a valuable tool for removing water sprouts. The teeth are wide-set and usually are pointed toward the operator. The blade is curved and can be attached to the pole at various angles, or the saw may be removed from the pole and used as a handsaw.

The ordinary carpenter's saw is not too good for cutting off living limbs because the teeth become so gummed up with the soft moist sawdust that they bind, whereas the pruning saws have "wide-set" teeth which make the cut wider than the thickness of the blade and so there is no danger of their becoming jammed.

Pruning saws vary in shape and size. You probably will decide that you need at least two—one with a narrow blade and one with a broad one. If you have a pole saw of the socket type, it can be detached from the pole and serve as a substitute for the saws which look like the small compass or keyhole saws used by carpenters. For cutting large limbs you can get a saw with a blade 24 or 28 inches long or you may prefer the bracket-type saw. This has the advantage of a detachable blade which can be removed for sharpening and a spare one may be put in its place. The kind illustrated can be set at any angle by loosening a thumbscrew. For larger work the one shown at top of page 24, which has a 30-inch blade, and which looks like a conventional carpenter's saw except for the teeth, can be used.

The tree expert's saw has the teeth pointing away from the operator. Many of the saws designed for pruning living wood have the teeth pointing in the opposite direction, toward the operator, so that they work on the downstroke. This is a big advantage, especially in the pole saws, because there is one strike against you— the pull of gravity, which is considerable—that must be overcome.

It is a good plan to see and handle these tools before making a purchase. It is essential, in the case of saws, that the opening in the handle be large enough to fit your hand, especially if you wear gloves when you are working.

Tools that are of occasional use include mattock, spade, and ax.

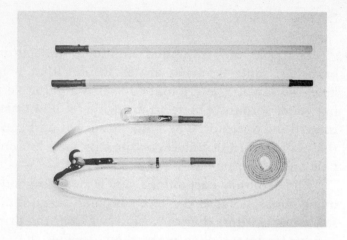

A combination tool. On the left is a pole pruner which can cut branches 1 inch in diameter if the blade is sharp. This can be converted to a pole saw by replacing the pruner with the saw attachment.

Pole saw used to remove a crossing branch.

Water sprouts being removed with a pole saw.

Pole saw used as a hand saw.

Close up of a pole saw. This one has straight teeth. The hole in the hook may be used to hold a swab or paintbrush for applying wound dressing.

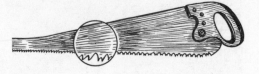

A good type of saw for cutting large limbs.

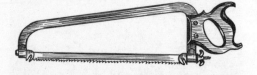

Bracket-type saw.

This double-edge saw has one objectionable feature in that the edge that is not being used may abrade nearby branches.

A mattock. A tool used to chop off suckers (see page 107).

A spade being used to cut off suckers of Raspberries. It may also be used for root pruning (see page 79) and trimming of underground parts of Germander (see page 267).

CHAPTER III

Plants Grown as "Standards"

IN THE lexicon of the gardener a "standard" plant is one grown to a single stem which, finally, is free from leaves and branches to a height of from 1 to 8 feet, or more, with a branching head at the top. The roses offered in catalogues as "tree" roses are familiar examples of plants grown to standard form, as also are the Weeping Mulberry and Umbrella Catalpa. Plants grown as standards have various uses in the garden. They are prized for giving accent to a composition and in formal gardens because, once they are made, they have a definite form and are more or less static, as they do not increase rapidly in size. They are sometimes used as "dot" plants in large beds of low-growing subjects, where they serve to break the flatness. In England, where standard roses are used much more freely than here, certain varieties are considered much less subject to mildew when thus grown.

There are three methods whereby standard plants are produced: (1) By grafting or budding upon a previously grown stem of the same or related species. (2) By cutting to the ground a plant which has been established a year or more and then allowing only one shoot to develop from the rootstock. (3) By starting from the seed or cutting stage and allowing only one shoot to develop until it has attained the required height.

Standards produced by grafting include such plants as "tree" Roses, budded on *Rosa rugosa*, (*R. canina* is commonly used for this purpose in England); Umbrella Catalpa is budded on *Catalpa speciosa;* Weeping Mulberry, budded or grafted on White Mulberry; Camperdown Elm on *Ulmus glabra;* Weeping Spring Cherry on *Prunus subhirtella;* and *Sophora japonica pendula* (Weeping Scholar Tree) on *S. japonica*. The Roses and Cherries are budded in July and August; Catalpa is budded in June—using buds from shoots kept dormant in cold storage; Mulberries may be grafted in April

Rose standards used as accents in a rose garden.

or budded in July; the Camperdown Elm is grafted in May or budded in August; and the Scholar Tree is grafted in the spring.

Unless you are familiar with the technique of budding and grafting and have suitable understocks available, perhaps it is better to purchase plants of this nature from a nursery rather than to attempt to "roll your own." Of course, if you are in no special hurry to obtain specimen standard plants and will not be discouraged if you have a few failures, go ahead and do your own grafting—you will find it full of interest. The techniques to be followed can be learned from almost any book on general gardening; from all books concerned with plant propagation; but best of all from visiting a nursery when grafting and budding is in progress.

Dwarf Catalpa is not handsome during the time it is dormant. These are pruned in late winter by cutting back the shoots, made the preceding year, to within an inch or two of their bases. Some of the stubs toward the center have died and should be sawed off.

The second method—that of cutting back an established plant and then allowing only one shoot to develop—does not demand any difficult technique and may be adopted with a large variety of plants. We have used it successfully with some of the climbing roses—Hiawatha, Miss Flora Mitten, and Ben Stad being the

Rose, Miss Flora Mitten, in the Rose Garden at the Brooklyn Botanic Garden. The shoots starting up from the base are to be eliminated.

ones which gave best results. Young plants are set out in spring or fall and allowed to grow at will for one year. The following spring the plant is cut down to the ground and, when it starts to grow, all shoots but the strongest one are rubbed off. The shoot that is left is supported by tying it to a stout stake. When this shoot has attained the required height its tip is pinched out to induce side buds to grow to form a head. The side shoots, in turn, have their tips pinched when they have attained a length of from 6 to 12 inches. When a sufficiently branching head has been acquired, further pinching is unnecessary. Of course, any shoots which originate on the stem below the head must be rubbed off as soon as they are discovered, except that, in the case of roses, if an additional strong shoot should develop from near the surface of the ground it is well to leave it as a reserve in case of accident to the first shoot.

The general procedure outlined above is applicable to many hardy woody plants. Among those suitable for standards but which may require permanent support for their main stem are Wisteria and Grape. Some are capable of self-support once the head has been formed. In this group we have such shrubs as Bush Honeysuckle, Peegee Hydrangea, Privet, and Azalea. When trees are grown as standards a bare stem of suitable height cannot be developed in one year and the training must be spread over several years. Maple and Linden are among the trees sometimes grown as standards with the top trimmed to a square or rectangular "head."

So far we have been dealing with hardy plants. Fuchsia, Heliotrope, Oleander, and Pelargonium can be trained as standards and are valuable for summer display outdoors, but, ideally, they should be stored in a greenhouse during the dormant season. If a greenhouse is not available a cool cellar kept between 35 and 45 degrees is an acceptable makeshift. When a cellar is used very little water should be given, thus making the plants go to rest to pass the winter in a more or less moribund condition.

The third method—that of starting the training in babyhood—is applicable to a variety of plants, Fuchsia, Heliotrope, Lantana, Pelargonium, and others, but is especially suitable for "one season" standards formed from Chrysanthemum, Coleus, Petunia, and Verbena. When following this method great judgment must be exercised in removing side shoots. The aim is to stimulate the

Rose. A single strong shoot has been selected and tied to a stout stake.

Unwanted shoots are being pulled off by thumb and finger.

Top has been cut back to encourage branching. All basal growth has been removed.

First blooms. Another shoot starting up from the base will be
conserved to take over in case of
the death of the original.

growth of the main shoot until it has attained the desired height,
and usually this is best accomplished by the complete removal of
all side shoots. But the plant must carry enough leaves to nourish
the roots. If the leaves on the main shoot are large and vigorous
they may be sufficient, but if they are not, the side shoots should
be allowed to grow a few inches before they are checked in order
to provide enough leaf surface. Later in the season, when the head
is being formed, the laterals below the head may be cut off close
to the main stem.

CHAPTER IV

Failure to Bloom or Bear

TREES and shrubs can produce flowers without setting a single fruit, but they cannot produce fruit without first having flowers.

There are numerous factors which may operate to inhibit the production of flowers; such as imbalance of nutrients in the soil (for example, overabundance of nitrogen), lack of nutrients, poor environment (for example, not enough sun), inadequate under-drainage of the soil, too much pruning, and extremely low temperatures. Severe cold can kill the flower buds even when the plants are completely dormant. Peach and Forsythia flowers may suffer when the temperature drops to below zero. This accounts for the failure of flower buds of Forsythia to develop on the upper part of the shrub while the lower part may bloom normally if it has been covered with snow.

The weather at blossoming time may play an important part, either directly or indirectly, in fruit production. It may be so miserable that bees do not venture out to do their job as pollinators, or heavy rains, when the flowers are open, may wash the pollen away.

Another point that must be recognized is that in many cases there is what is known as "self-incompatibility," which demands cross-pollination to insure fruit production.

Then there are dioecious plants, which produce male and female flowers on separate plants. Holly is an example.

Pruning must not be done at the wrong season. As an example, most varieties of *Hydrangea macrophylla* ("French" Hydrangea) produce their flowers only from the tips of the shoots made the preceding year; if these are cut off early in the spring or if they are killed by low temperatures during the winter, they cannot blossom.

Pruning during the late summer may result in sappy growth which can be affected by low temperature; similarly, the same effect may be produced if the subject is grown in soil that is too rich. For example, *Cytisus scoparius* (Scotch Broom) and *Kolkwitzia amabilis* (Beauty Bush) when grown in poor sandy soil may come through the winter with no damage, but if grown in rich soil may be killed to the ground.

Summer pruning may hurry up the blossoming of some varieties of Apple and Pear, especially in the case of espaliered plants.

If, after five or six years, Apples show no sign of blossoming except for notoriously laggard varieties such as Baldwin and Northern Spy, which are slow in coming to bear, something must be done about it. When trees are growing vigorously the elimination of nitrogen in the fertilizer program and/or the planting of a cover crop of Winter Rye, Rye Grass, or Buckwheat in August may, by checking the exuberant vegetative growth, cause the trees to produce blossoms. If neither of these measures is successful root pruning should be tackled. This is done by digging a trench 1½ to 2 feet deep halfway around the tree, 3 to 6 feet from the trunk, and cutting off the large roots encountered. The trenches should not be continuous. First make a circle around the tree and divide it into four or six equal parts, alternating trench with undisturbed areas. Mix superphosphate, ½ pound to each square yard, with the soil before filling it back into the trenches. Avoid pruning the top of the trees when they are dormant, and if they still persist in making luxuriant shoot growth, the other half of the root system should be pruned.

CHAPTER V

Hedges

HEDGES may be formal or informal. A formal hedge is one that is pruned with hedge shears to keep it to the desired form and size, while an informal hedge is allowed to grow more or less naturally with just enough pruning with one-hand shears or lopping shears to keep it within bounds.

One important thing to remember with hedge plants is to prevent them from growing up too fast. This can be accomplished by cutting them back moderately as soon as they are planted and by

Two kinds of hedge. In the rear is *Ligustrum ovalifolium* (California Privet). Next is *Euonymus alatus compactus*. The low-growing edging is English Ivy.

Hedera helix (English Ivy) can be used as a hedge when provided with a suitable support. It is pruned by an over-all shearing when the growth is about to start in the spring, supplemented by shortening, with secateurs, sufficient shoots during the growing season to keep the hedge from getting out of bounds.

Instead of making a solid hedge, supports may be such that openings are left.

Taxus baccata (English Yew). When I first saw this hedge about sixty years ago, it was about 10 feet high. It is now about 6 feet, having been cut back severely a few years before the picture was taken.

nipping the tips of the shoots whenever they attain the length of 8 to 10 inches. This is heartbreaking to the owner of the hedge, but he will be repaid in later years by having a hedge furnished from top to bottom, whereas, if left unpruned, the growth toward the bottom of the hedge would be sparse and spotty. Also, the trimming should be done in such a way that the hedge is narrower at the top than at the bottom.

It may sometimes be necessary to cut a hedge almost to the ground if it has grown too large for the position it occupies. But do not do this unless there is a reasonable certainty that it is a species that is amenable to such cutting back. The following are known to break from old wood even when they are cut back severely: Boxwood, *Euonymus, Ilex aquifolium, I. opaca,* and, among the deciduous ones, *Acanthopanax, Crataegus,* and the ubiquitous California Privet.

The dwarf hedge, *Lonicera nitida,* is not winter-hardy in climates where the temperature falls below 25 degrees. The hedge on the right is *Taxus baccata.*

Among the plants which make satisfactory hedges are the following:

EVERGREENS

Broad-Leaf

Berberis julianae, B. verruculosa. These need very little pruning. Merely cut back any shoots that spoil their symmetry. Set them about two feet apart.

Euonymus fortunei vegetus and the new Corliss varieties which have been distinguished by the prefix "Emerald" are excellent hedge material. Noteworthy varieties are Emerald Charm and Emerald Leader (see page 38 for other varieties). Emerald Charm should be set from 1 to 2 feet apart. Emerald Leader can be set 2 to 3 feet apart. Shorten new shoots to make the hedge more compact.

Chamaecyparis obtusa compacta. Plant 2 to 3 feet apart. Not much pruning is necessary. Merely cut off shoots which are exceeding the bounds.

Poncirus (Citrus) *trifoliata.* This is really a deciduous species, but its stems are green throughout the year and thus it is, in effect, an evergreen. It is not reliably hardy in regions that have winters more rugged than Long Island, New York. It makes an impenetrable spiny hedge, especially if given a light over-all shearing during July. Space 3 or 4 feet apart.

Ilex crenata (see page 135). Shear to shorten the new growth in July. If the shoots have been injured by winter they should be cut off in the spring. Use *crenata* for a large hedge of 8 feet or more. If a 2- to 3-foot hedge is desired use one of the dwarf varieties, *helleri, convexa,* or *globosa.*

Ilex opaca (American Holly), *I. aquifolium* (English Holly), *I. cornuta* (Chinese Holly) and its variety *I. c. burfordi* excel as hedges in regions where they are hardy. Set them from 2 to 4 feet apart. They may be expected to reach a height of 10 or more feet if required or they may be kept to 3 to 5 feet, shearing them twice, once in the spring when new growth is starting and again in July to shorten new shoots.

Ilex glabra (Inkberry) has the merit of being perfectly hardy. The fly in the ointment is its tendency toward legginess. But this can be controlled by pruning when young.

Ilex vomitoria (Yaupon) and *I. cassine* (Dahoon) are suitable for planting in the mild winter climates of Virginia and southward. Space them 2 to 3 feet apart.

Buxus sempervirens suffruticosa (Dwarf Box) in restored Williamsburg.

Boxwood is capable of making a close-knit hedge or edging but it needs yearly care. There used to be a walk between the rows of Boxwood in this picture. It should be sheared early in the spring and again toward the end of June.

Euonymus fortunei Emerald Charm is a kind that should be chosen if a narrow hedge is required.

Euonymus fortunei Emerald Leader is an excellent type to use in making a formal hedge. Because it is almost as broad as it is tall, fewer plants will be needed.

Ilex opaca (American Holly) used as a hedge in Williamsburg, Virginia.

American Holly is used to form a maze in the garden at the Governor's Palace in restored Williamsburg.

Narrow-Leaf

Abies species (Fir), *Picea* species (Spruce). These two may be spaced 2 to 3 feet apart according to the size of the plants. They should be pruned by trimming the young shoots, usually in July when they have attained their full growth.

Pinus strobus (White Pine) is good for use when a tall-growing (up to 10 feet or more) hedge is required. *Pinus mugo* (Swiss Mountain Pine) is excellent for a low-growing hedge. *Pinus sylvestris* (Scots Pine) is a good choice when the soil is poor and sandy. All of these pines can be pruned by shortening the "candles" in the spring; also by cutting them back to a first whorl or, when the objective is to reduce the size, to the second whorl.

Taxus (Yew) is probably the most satisfactory of all evergreen hedges. It seems to be indifferent to soil conditions, is easily transplanted, will grow in the shade, and breaks well from old wood. All Yews should be pruned by shearing in July and again in the spring before growth starts.

Taxus baccata (English Yew) is a species with many garden forms. Except for the variety *repandens,* which seems to be as hardy as the Japanese Yew, it is not reliable in climates more severe than that of Long Island, New York.

Taxus cuspidata (Japanese Yew) is the one that is most commonly used for hedgemaking.

Taxus media—a hybrid between *T. cuspidata* and *T. baccata*— includes two varieties, *T. hatfieldi* and *T. hicksi,* which because of their columnar growth habit are particularly valuable where a tall, narrow hedge is required.

Thuja occidentalis (American Arborvitae) is excellent as an evergreen hedge for planting in an exposed location. It may be sheared in spring when growth is about to begin and again, if necessary, during midsummer.

Thuja orientalis (Oriental Arborvitae) because of its habit of growth is not so successful as the native species. With many shoots starting from the base it is likely to be injured by snow. When it is grown as a specimen it is advisable to tie the branches together by fastening a piece of tape to a strong branch near the ground line, winding it around and around in a spiral, and fastening the

Taxus cuspidata (Japanese Yew). Two barbers at work giving a hedge its Fourth of July bob. The pyramidal specimen on the right is a form of *Taxus media*. One pruning about midsummer is all that is necessary until the hedge approaches the limit in size. Then two or three clippings a year may be needed to keep it within bounds—one before growth starts in the spring, the second about mid-June, and the third in early August.

end to a strong branch in the upper part of the plant. This should be done in late fall or early winter. If grown as a hedge it can be protected by putting stakes alongside of the hedge and connecting them with strong twine.

Tsuga canadensis (Hemlock) is probably the most satisfactory of all evergreen hedges when the cost of planting is considered. Plants may be set 2 to 3 feet apart in the spring and given an over-all shearing at once. Subsequent pruning is carried out during June or July to shorten the new growth.

DECIDUOUS

Acanthopanax pentaphyllus (Five-leaved Aralia) is valuable chiefly because it will grow almost anywhere in full shade or in sun. When used as a hedge it should be clipped when the new growth has been made in the spring. The flowers are inconspicuous and can be ignored.

Tsuga canadensis (Hemlock). This hedge was planted in 1916. It illustrates the effect of annual shearing as a means of limiting growth.

The Hemlock shown here was planted at the same time as the hedge in the preceding picture and was allowed to grow naturally.

Acanthopanax sieboldianus (*A. pentaphyllus*) need not be made to look like the busbies worn by some of the English regiments. It can be used as a solid hedge.

Berberis thunbergi (Japanese Barberry) and its varieties *B. t. minor, B. t. compacta,* and *B. t. pluriflora* (Columnberry) are, for the most part, excellent for informal hedges, especially when a thorny, impervious barrier is required. Very little pruning is necessary, except that the variety *minor* needs to be sheared at least once a year when it is used as an edging. The straight species *B. thunbergi* is capable of growing to 8 feet tall and as much or more in diameter, so if you are limited for space you should concentrate on variety *compacta* or variety *pluriflora.*

Berberis mentorensis (Mentor Barberry), a hybrid between *B. thunbergi* and *B. julianae,* is magnificent in the fall, when its foliage changes to a very strong red (Nickerson Colorfan). It is a good choice where an informal hedge 6 feet high is required. Although it is said to be evergreen in mild climates, here in the mid-Hudson Valley it is deciduous. Prune by cutting back wayward shoots.

Chaenomeles lagenaria (Japanese Quince) and varieties. The one known as *C. l.* Spitfire is an upright-grower suitable where a narrow hedge is required. When it is used for formal accent it is advisable to tie it to a stake. Pruning consists of shortening the shoots during the growing season. This can be done by thumb and finger or, if a hedge is concerned, by using hedge shears. Set the plants about 2 or 3 feet apart.

Euonymus alatus and *E. a. compactus.* Neither of these requires any pruning except when it becomes necessary to keep their height down. To do this it is advisable to cut them back in July and if necessary, they can be cut back again into the old wood the following spring. They are subject to attack by a black aphid which causes the topmost leaves to curl. Because of the difficulty of reaching them by contact spray, the most satisfactory way of fighting this pest is to cut off the affected tips as soon as they are visible. The variety *compactus* is better fitted for a small hedge than *alatus.*

Rosa rugosa (Ramanas Rose), *R. hugonis* (Father Hugo's Rose), and *R. multiflora* (Japanese Rose) are perhaps the most popular species used in hedgemaking. They are best used in an informal way by limiting the pruning to cutting out, annually, a few of the older stems during the late winter. Sometimes it becomes desirable to prune drastically by cutting the entire bush almost to the ground line. *Rosa multiflora* is not a good plant for a hedge where space is limited, because it grows much too large.

Vaccinium corymbosum (High-bush Blueberry). If soil conditions are right—moist and acid—a Blueberry hedge can double in brass in being useful as well as ornamental. See under "Fruits" for pruning methods. At least two varieties should be used to insure cross-pollination.

Other plants which can be used for hedges include *Lonicera fragrantissima* (Bush Honeysuckle), *L. morrowi* (Morrow Honeysuckle), *L. tatarica* (Tartarian Honeysuckle), *Malus atrosanguinea* (Carmine Crabapple), *M. floribunda* (Showy Crabapple), *M. ioensis* (Prairie Crabapple), many other Crabapples, and *Crataegus* (Hawthorn or Thornapple). For the first year or so after they are planted the side shoots should be checked by heading them back. Once this has been done, an over-all shearing when the new growth is almost finished, usually in June or July, is sufficient.

CHAPTER VI

Topiary—Pleached Allée—Bonsai

Topiary

No matter how much we decry the practice of training and pruning plants into bizarre shapes, we must admit that it has the sanction of age. Topiary was known to the Romans and it is still to be found not only in England and the European continent but also in America, and not only at restored Williamsburg. One great example in the eastern United States is the topiary garden on the Hunnewell Estate at Wellesley, Massachusetts, but in general the art of clipping bushes into geometrical or other figures is somewhat passé. However, at the Chelsea Show of the Royal Horticultural Society in 1956 there was an exhibit by Kew Topiary, Ltd., a firm which specializes in topiary work. I missed the

A garden of topiary at the Hunnewell estate, Wellesley, Massachusetts.

Topiary at the Chelsea Show, 1956. Two standard Bay trees with a pyramid between them, an excellent corkscrew, and a begging French poodle in the right foreground.

well-named house of Cutbush ("Cutbushes by Cutbushes"), now no longer in existence, which used to exhibit wonderful specimens of topiary work about fifty years ago at the Temple Show, the forerunner of the Chelsea Show.

The first thing to be done is to select the plant material which will ultimately be sculptured. The plants must be amenable to shearing and training, easily transplanted, and winter-hardy in the region where they are to be grown, and the sculptor must be patient. Among the plants which are first-class material for this purpose are *Taxus cuspidata* (Japanese Yew), *Buxus sempervirens* and its variety *suffruticosa* (Dwarf Box), *Tsuga canadensis* (Hemlock), and *Taxus baccata* (English Yew). *T. baccata* is not reliably hardy in northeastern states, with the exception of the variety *repandens* and to a somewhat lesser degree the hybrid *Taxus media* (*T. cuspidata* ✕

T. baccata). Boxwood cannot be relied on in the regions that have more severe winters than Washington, D.C. Another plant which does not resent close clipping, though not evergreen in severe climates, is *Ligustrum ovalifolium* (California Privet). Other privets, such as *L. japonicum* (Wax Privet) and *L. lucidum* (Shiny Privet), are evergreen but not reliably hardy north of Virginia. Among the trees which can endure severe pruning year after year are *Platanus acerifolia* (London Plane), *Tilia cordata* (Small-leaved Linden), *T. euchlora* (a hybrid form), and *T. europaea* (Common Linden, Basswood, or Lime). The leaves of these, however, are too large for making grotesque and intricate geometrical figures. But I have seen them with a clean trunk up to 8 feet, trimmed to a cubelike head.

Another view of the same exhibit. Incongruous elements are the tubbed "French" Hydrangeas in the foreground.

Topiary in the garden of Mr. Claude C. Jacobs, Surrey, England. Notice the clipped Yew hedge back of the seat.

Topiary in the making. Clipped Yaupon Holly at Chiswell House, Williamsburg, Virginia.

Not exactly topiary, but a clipped Crabapple shows that this variety, *Malus atrosanguinea,* can endure close clipping without loss of flowers.

Not topiary, strictly speaking. A foundation planting kept from growing too large by frequent shearing during the growing season.

Pleached allée of American Beech at Williamsburg, Virginia. View of the outside.

Pleached Allée

Not everyone has room for a pleached arbor or allée, at least not on the scale that it is done in restored Williamsburg. Usually best results are obtained when trees are trained on a metal or wood framework. Trees suitable for this purpose are Beech, Hornbeam, Buttonwood, and fruits such as Peach, Pear, or Apple. They can be grown to single or double cordons or they may be fan-trained.

The dimensions should be in accordance with the scale of the property. I would suggest that for the average-sized place 8 feet high by 7 feet wide would be the minimum, and it should be appropriately placed in a position where it will be useful. For example, it can connect the house and the garage or the dwelling with a garden feature such as a piece of statuary, a seat, or whatever it is you have. Whenever possible it should be oriented to run

View of the inside.

north and south so that the plants on each side have an equal chance.

The plants should be set 2 or 3 feet apart and cut almost to the ground. The strong shoots that will be stimulated by the pruning should be tied to the framework, spacing them as equally as possible. Subsequent pruning will be directed toward filling any vacant places on the framework by cutting back to a shoot or bud that is pointing in the right direction, and then cutting off superfluous shoots. When the shoots on both sides mingle they may be pleached, or plashed (woven together), so that eventually they may become grafted one to another. The support may be removed, if desired, as soon as this stage is reached.

To most gardeners the making of a pleached allée or arbor is of purely academic interest, so that is all I am going to say about it here.

Bonsai

Bonsai is the name given by the Japanese to dwarfed trees grown in containers. One of the difficulties in most parts of the United States is how to carry them over the winter. They must be kept cool enough to avoid the possibility of their starting to grow before winter is over and warm enough to avoid the danger of frost breaking the containers, some of which may be valuable. If you have a deep cold frame, a greenhouse, or an enclosed porch in which the temperature averages about 45 degrees during the winter with artificial heat that will prevent the temperature from going below 30 degrees and in the other direction not more than 60 degrees and have the urge to grow Bonsai, you will be justified in making an attempt.

First you should familiarize yourself with the type of plant material favored by the Japanese by visiting someone in your neighborhood who has a collection. Next consider the plant material you plan to use. Some of this can be dug up from the wild or

This plant already has had several years of training, as witness the branches that have been trained to grow a complete circle. It now needs additional pruning.

The right side has been pruned. The left side is being pruned.

Pruning completed.

you may be able to find suitable plants in your local nursery which you should be able to obtain at reduced prices because they are not symmetrical enough to warrant their sale as specimen plants. Among suitable evergreens are the following: *Pinus sylvestris* (Scots Pine), *P. mughus* (Swiss Mountain Pine), *Tsuga canadensis* (Hemlock), and *Chamaecyparis obtusa* (Hinoki Cypress). The deciduous flowering trees sometimes used include *Prunus subhirtella* (Spring Cherry), *P. serrulata* (Japanese Flowering Cherry), and *P. persica* (Peach).

Plants to be dwarfed are sometimes dug up from the wild and potted or planted out in the cold frame. To compensate for the loss of roots, the tops are carefully cut back, making the first steps in shaping up the plant so that it begins to attain the form you

New quarters are being prepared for the Zelkova tree. Notice the wires which are passed through the drainage holes.

Ready for placement.

desire. The following year they will probably be fit to plant in their permanent containers. These should be shallow with holes in the bottom for drainage.

Tree in place and new soil is being packed around and over the roots.

The tree is held securely in the container by the copper wire shown in first picture.

Potting completed, dried and powdered green moss is being sprinkled on the surface. This is the common green moss (*Funaria hygrometrica*), including lichen, which usually grows on rocks.

CHAPTER VII

Pruning Understocks of Grafted Plants

WHEN grafting is done (either scion or bud) it usually is necessary to prune the understock after the graft has "taken" (united with the understock).

For example: In the case of Rhododendron, when a side graft is used, the union takes place in three or four weeks and the top half of the understock is then cut off. A few weeks later, when the callus has changed its color to a deep brown, another inch or so of the understock is cut off and a few weeks later the remainder of the understock can be removed, making the cut just above the union. Blue Spruce, *Picea pungens* Koster, is grafted on an understock of *P. abies* (Norway Spruce). These are grafted in a propagating frame in a greenhouse beginning late in February or early in March. The potted understock, just prior to grafting, is cut back to leave it about 8 to 10 inches tall. When the scion starts growing, 2 or 3 inches more of the understock are cut off. Toward the end of May a further reduction of the understock is made. Part of it is left until the end of the growing season, when the remainder is removed.

Grafting is usually done on one- or two-year-old understocks, but if a scion of a different variety is grafted in a mature tree—as, for example, when a Pink-flowering Dogwood is grafted in a white-flowering form or when a male shoot is grafted on a female plant of Holly to insure pollination—it is necessary to make sure that the grafted portion is not smothered by the growth of the host plant. This is done by cutting off any shoots that are encroaching, and when the grafted portion has made enough growth to encourage the sap to flow in its direction, the understock is cut off just above the point of union.

In the case of the Dogwood, neighboring portions of the white-flowering understock are cut back so that the graft has a chance to become dominant.

Blue Spruce grafted on Norway Spruce. Center understock ready to be cut off, at arrow. Left—further reduction of understock in May, at arrow. Right— remainder of understock removed.

Suckers from Grafted Plants

We are constantly getting letters from beginning gardeners who complain that their beautiful red Rose has changed to one which has only small white flowers in large bunches. The explanation of this is that the understock on which the red Rose was grafted, usually by budding, has grown at the expense of the grafted Rose. This means that you should be suspicious of any shoots which originate below the ground. Usually these shoots have leaves which possess seven or more leaflets as contrasted with the five leaflets that are usual on Hybrid Tea Roses. If it is noticed soon enough it may be possible to pull it up in its entirety, but all too often it is not seen early enough, with the result that you have to cut it off with pruning shears and that means that it will start growing again. Then it may be a case of digging up the entire plant, sepa-rating the understock, and replanting the rose that you want to

A *multiflora* understock can be identified by its strong growth as compared with that of the grafted Rose.

Cutting out an unwanted understock of Rose. Even during the winter it is often possible to distinguish the understock from the graft by the character of the thorns.

Merely cutting off the understock was not enough in this case, so in the fall the entire ensemble was dug up and separated—understock at left, graft at right.

keep. This should be done either in the spring before growth starts or in the fall.

Other plants which are commonly propagated by grafting include *Viburnum carlesi*, *Paeonia suffruticosa* (Tree Peony), and *Cornus florida rubra* (Pink-flowering Dogwood). Close watch must be kept on these, and if the understock is growing it should be eliminated immediately.

Sometimes it is more convenient to cut off the unwanted portion with a saw.

Sometimes lopping shears can be used, as here.

A gnarled portion of an understock. The result of several abortive attempts to get rid of it by cutting off the aboveground parts.

CHAPTER VIII

Pruning Roses

NOVICES often are unduly worried when the time comes to prune Roses, thinking they may prune too much or too little. It may help to remove this mental hazard, so far as Hybrid Tea Roses and related kinds are concerned, when it is known that there are two widely divergent schools of thought—one believing in severe pruning, which involves cutting the plants down to within a few inches of the ground each year, the other insisting that this is a barbarous practice and that the better plan is to cut the bushes back as little as possible. Good results are obtained by both methods. Much depends on the objectives. If exhibition roses are required, severe pruning is usually needed; if a large quantity of flowers is preferred for garden display, light pruning is indicated. Personally, I am on the side of the moderates, believing that the bushes will be healthier and live longer when the pruning is not too drastic. With these preliminary observations, let's get down to business and assess the job in general and in particular.

Pruning When Planting

Many nurserymen prune Roses before shipping so that they are ready to plant when received. If this has not been done, the first step is to cut off the mangled root tips—preferably with a sharp knife. Then cut off weak, twiggy shoots about the base. Further pruning in the case of Tea, Hybrid Tea, Dwarf Polyantha, Floribunda, Grandiflora, and Hybrid Perpetual Roses consists of cutting back the remaining canes to between 6 and 12 inches from the base of the plant, the severity of the pruning depending on the vigor of the plant—the weaker it is, the more it is pruned.

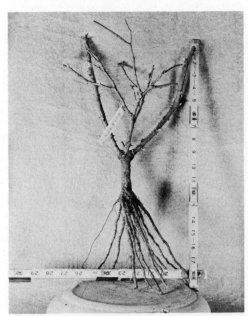

A Rose as received from the nursery. The twiggy growth in the center should be removed.

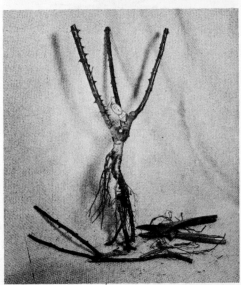

Rose similar to one shown above has been pruned and is ready for planting.

Climbing Roses of all types should have twiggy growth removed and the remaining canes cut back to half their length. Shrub Roses need broken branches and those which spoil the symmetry of the bush removed, and one-year-old shoots should be shortened about one half.

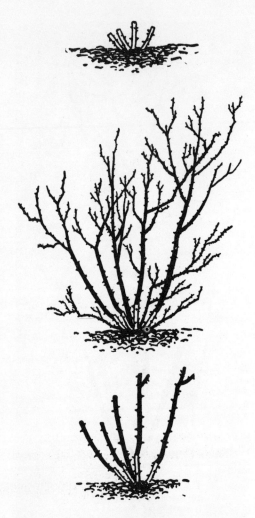

Around the year with a moderate-growing Hybrid Tea. Top, in the spring the newly planted bush was pruned back to stubs. Center, strong growth (black) quickly developed from buds on stubs and flowered in the summer; also, one strong shoot and three weaker ones grew from the base of the bush at ground level or below. Bottom, the bush pruned early the next spring.

Pruning Established Roses

When? In the spring for most classes (exceptions later) when new shoots are about ¼ inch long. The questioning beginner may ask, "Do not these shoots use food materials stored in roots and stems, which is lost when they are cut off?" The answer is "Yes," but Roses start to grow too early for their own good, and the new shoots are sometimes killed by late frosts. If they are pruned before growth starts, the lower buds are forced to grow, and if these are killed, there are few or none to take their place.

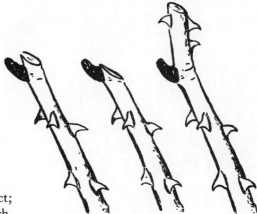

Pruning to a bud. Left, correct;
center, too close; right, too high.

How? First cut off all dead and injured wood. Dead wood is brown and dry; the inner bark of injured wood may be green, sappy, and apparently normal on the outside, but the pith is dark brown and shriveled. The buds on such shoots may make a growth of several inches and then suddenly collapse. This is a common occurrence, which usually can be attributed to winter injury undiscerned at the time of pruning. If you live in the North, when you have cut off dead and injured wood, your pruning will be finished, so far as the varieties (Tea and Hybrid Tea) least resistant to severe freezing are concerned. When there is a lot of top growth left after dead wood has been removed, further procedures are regulated by the class to which the Rose belongs and the purpose in view.

When shortening canes, make the cut just above a bud pointing in the direction you wish to have the shoot grow. Usually an outward-pointing bud is chosen to avoid crossing branches. The cut should be about ¼ inch above the bud and slope slightly away from it. When removing old, worn-out branches from near the base, cut as close as possible to the parent branch.

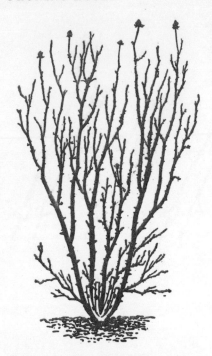

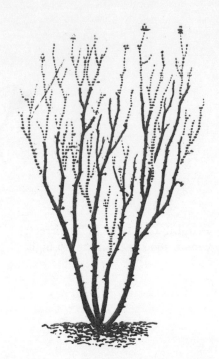

Strong-growing Hybrid Tea. Most of first year's growth (black) from base.

Same bush after light pruning (dotted lines) for many flowers. Stubs removed.

Tea and Hybrid Tea

First take a good look at the bush. If there are branches which are rough and gnarled and carry none but thin weak twigs, cut them off close to the parent branch. Except when dealing with old neglected bushes, there may be only one or two of these, or maybe none. Then cut off any thin, weak shoots and cut back the strong remaining shoots one third of their length if your objective is many flowers; one half to two thirds if you prefer large but fewer flowers.

Climbing Hybrid Tea

These are vigorous sports of the bush-type Hybrid Tea Roses. Pruning should be kept to a minimum. All that is necessary is to cut out dead and worn-out shoots and to shorten or remove weak, twiggy shoots.

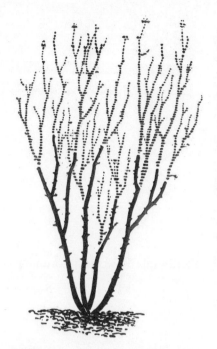 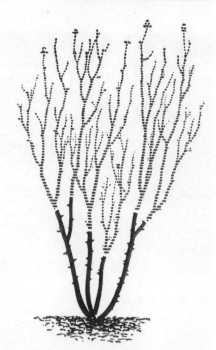

| Moderate pruning results in somewhat larger, but generally fewer, blossoms. | For real exhibition-size blooms, in reduced numbers, prune the bush severely. |

Dwarf Polyantha and Floribunda

Ordinarily these need but little pruning beyond cutting back, lightly, the shoots that have bloomed and occasionally removing near the ground line some of the oldest and least vigorous branches. There are some who practice cutting back the Small-flowered Polyanthas almost to the ground every year when they wish to keep them within a certain height.

Hybrid Perpetuals

There are two distinct methods of handling this group. One is to treat them essentially in the same way as Hybrid Teas, except that because of their usually more vigorous growth they are seldom cut back more than one third. The other method is practicable when the variety has the habit of producing new canes from the

Floribunda Rose before pruning.

Same Rose after pruning.

Floribunda Rose showing placement of bloom in candelabra shape. The central flower, which was the first to bloom, can be cut with a stem 3 to 6 inches long without removing any buds.

A large bed of Frau Karl Druschki with branches tied down to pegs driven in the soil.

This picture shows numerous buds forced into growth by the horizontal position of the canes.

base and the bushes are widely spaced. It consists of taking the long shoots which grew the preceding year, bending them over in a wide arc, and fastening the tips to pegs driven in the ground. The semi-horizontal position forces buds to grow which otherwise would have remained dormant and results in a large number of blooms. Future pruning consists of the removal at the ground line of a sufficient number of the oldest canes to make room for the new shoots. A saw with a narrow blade (a keyhole saw) is a handy tool when cutting off old gnarled branches.

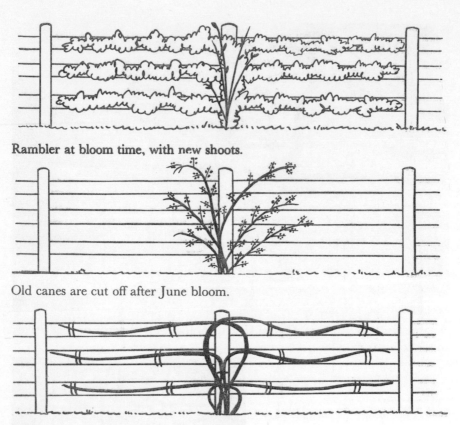

Rambler at bloom time, with new shoots.

Old canes are cut off after June bloom.

Later, new canes are tied up for the winter.

Rambler Roses

These blossom best on short side shoots (laterals) developed on the long, unbranched canes which grew the preceding year. They bear small flowers in large clusters and can be distinguished from the group to which the name "Climbers" is applied by numerous strong shoots originating at the base of the bush which at blooming time are 3 feet or more long. (Dorothy Perkins is perhaps the best known Rambler.) I prefer to prune this group just as soon as the flowers have faded, by cutting off at the ground line all canes which have flowered. The strong young canes, as many as are needed, are then tied up on the support. The remainder, if any, are cut off. If this was not done during August, it should be done in the fall or in the spring, and any shriveled cane tips cut off.

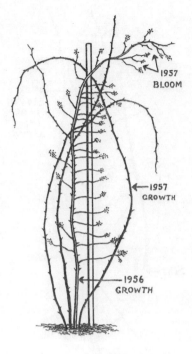

Rambler Rose cane (white) that grew in 1956 and flowered in 1957 is removed in the summer of 1957 or the spring of 1958.

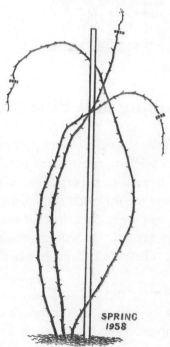

Canes that grew in 1957 tipped in the spring of 1958.

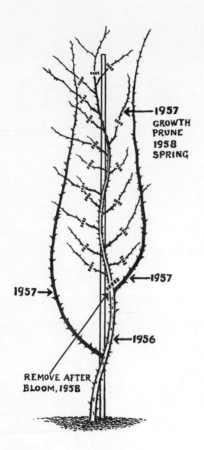

1957
GROWTH
PRUNE
1958
SPRING

←1957

1957→

←1956

REMOVE AFTER
BLOOM, 1958

Climbing Rose (for clarity only
one cane is shown). White cane
grew in 1956, branched and
flowered in 1957; prune small
laterals for 1958 bloom. Black
canes will take a similar course
in 1958 and 1959.

Climbing and Pillar Roses

These have a more permanent superstructure. Strong new
shoots seldom grow from the base of the plant but instead come
from branches several feet from the ground. Spring pruning, in
the case of old, well-established plants, consists of the removal of
worn-out branches (recognized by rough, dark bark and weak,
twiggy growth) by cutting them back to the ground or to a strong
shoot. The side branches which produced flowers last year are cut
back to a length of 3 to 9 inches. Summer pruning consists of
shortening new shoots which are exceeding their bounds. The
necessity for this should be avoided as much as possible by planting
strong-growing Roses, such as Dr. Van Fleet, only where there is
plenty of room for them to develop.

Rosa eglanteria (rubiginosa) (Sweet-briar Rose), showing old wood (dark stems) and new shoots (light-colored stems). Some of the old stems have been cut back. Further pruning needed is indicated by arrows.

Shrub and Species Roses

These include the Sweetbriar hybrids, the Rugosa hybrids, and species such as *Rosa hugonis* (Father Hugo's Rose), *R. rugosa* (Ramanas Rose), *R. spinosissima* (Scotch Rose), and others. Little pruning is necessary or desirable beyond the removal of dead branches. If the bush becomes unduly crowded, a few of the older and less vigorous branches may be removed, either by cutting them off at the ground line or by cutting back to a point where a strong new shoot is growing. The method chosen depends on which best serves for the maintenance of the natural habit and symmetry of the bush.

A Hybrid Tea Rose before and after disbudding. It would have been better had this been done when the buds were smaller.

Summer Pruning of Roses

Pruning bush Roses during the growing season is chiefly concerned with the removal of flowers for decoration and exhibition and the thinning out of their buds. This is a case where it is essential to know something of the habits of Roses in the various groups. Tea Roses and the Hybrid Teas that were introduced twenty or more years ago usually produce their flowers on fairly long stems with one to three flower buds on each. If there is one flower almost open and the buds are showing color, it is better to leave the largest bud, pinching out the other one. Roses for indoor use should be cut with the stalk long enough to serve its purpose as a cut flower and at the same time leave two or three growth buds.

If, however, the Roses are intended for exhibition, all the flower buds except one in each cluster are pinched off as soon as they are large enough to be handled. This must be done early; otherwise the wounds can plainly be seen and the judges will mark them as demerits.

In the case of those varieties which make candelabra-like flowering stems (many of the modern Hybrid Teas and the Floribunda and Dwarf Polyantha groups), the central flower in the

A grafted Rose (left) with understock (right) taking over.

The grafted Rose has been separated from the understock and is ready to be replanted.

cluster is the first to open. This should be removed, usually with about 2 or 3 inches of stem. The buds remaining will open almost at the same time, making a good show in the garden.

The length of the stem to be cut when pruning in the growing season depends in part on the purpose of the pruner. If he wants a good showing in the garden, he should not cut the flowers with long stems, but if he wants quality rather than quantity, they should be cut with fairly long stems, leaving no more than two or three growth buds on the current shoots.

When garden Roses are budded on *Rosa multiflora,* Ragged Robin, or Dr. Huey during July or August, some of them may start into growth the same season the bud was inserted. In this case the understock can be cut off right away. Usually, however, the scion (bud) remains dormant over the first winter. In the spring the understock is cut back as soon as the scions are showing new growth. Be sure it is the wanted Rose that grows and not the understock.

In preparing Roses for winter, if they are exposed to strong winds it is advisable to prune those which have made heavy shoots to shorten them; otherwise the constant whipping by winter winds may abrade the stems where they emerge from the ground.

The understock, *Rosa multiflora*
variety, has taken over completely.

1. Composted manure, plus peat moss or leaf mold if the soil is heavy, is dug
into the bottom of the hole. 2. Prior to planting any Rose, examine roots for
dead and broken portions. Cut off cleanly to live white wood. Spread roots
well over a mound of soil and sift soil among them. 3. Arrow points to one
typical weak stem that should be pruned back to strong main cane. In general, only three or, at most four, good canes should be left at planting. 4. If
main canes of thinned plant before planting are in good condition above
point indicated by arching broken line, they may be only moderately trimmed.
Otherwise cut back to point of line. 5. In the process of filling around roots
with good fertile soil, make sure that swelling of "bud" or graft will be just
below final level of soil after plant is firmed in place. 6. Roots must be put in
very firm contact with surrounding soil. Hence when they are well covered,
step into planting hole to pack soil. If job is done right, "bud" will be in correct position. 7. After tramping soil, fill rest of hole with water if ground is
dry at planting time. When hole has drained, fill with loose, dry soil to final
level. 8. Final step in planting is mounding up base of canes to depth of from
4 to 8 inches with clean soil, free from large lumps. If planting in spring, leave
in place for at least ten days, then pull it away from canes gradually. In fall
planting, it is left until the spring. 9. After ground is thoroughly warm and
plant established (mid-to-late May), it is helpful to mulch surface with peat
moss or similar porous material. This keeps down weeds, keeps roots cool and
moist during heat. 10. In cutting Roses for the house, or after blooms have
faded, leave at least two sets of five-part leaves for later bloom. The more
foliage you leave on plant, the healthier it is likely to be, this year and after.
11. Some gardeners cut back plants at approximately this line after peak of
June bloom. In general this gains nothing, may be harmful. However, strag-
gling growth should be removed before winter winds and snows.

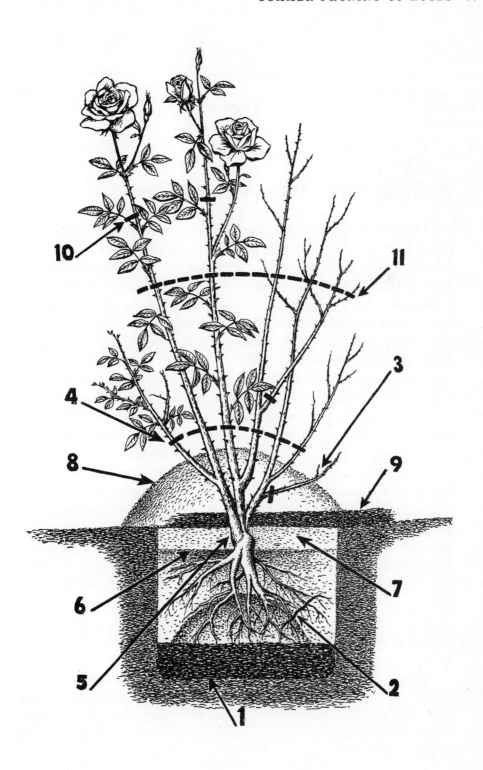

CHAPTER IX

Trees

Pruning When Transplanting Trees

Except when material consists of plants already established in containers, it is necessary to prune the tops in order to compensate for loss of roots, which is inevitable when the plants are dug from the open ground. Usually very little pruning is necessary when transplanting trees dug with a ball of earth. Nursery-grown trees, when they have been properly cared for by the nurseryman, can be planted with greater chance of success than those dug up from the wild. The reason for this is that in a well-managed nursery the plants are either transplanted or root-pruned at intervals of two or three years to promote a fibrous root system near the stem of the plant, whereas, when plants are growing wild, the roots spread so widely that it is not practicable to dig them with sufficient fibrous roots. If, for any reason, it is necessary to transfer a plant that has been growing in one place undisturbed for a number of years, it is advisable to root-prune it a year or two ahead of transplanting. This can be done by thrusting a spade into the ground in a circle around it so that many of the roots are cut. This promotes branching and the formation of numerous fibrous roots. In some cases when it is necessary that the root ball be more than 2 feet in diameter, it is preferable to dig a trench around the tree, cutting off the roots encountered. Then, for every square yard of surface, mix a 2- or 3-inch layer of moist Peat Moss and a half pound of superphosphate with the soil and fill it back into the trench.

When the tree is a sizable one, say 10 to 15 feet tall, it is often more convenient to do the pruning at the time of transplanting *before* the tree is put into the ground. First trim the ends of jagged roots. Then prune the top by taking out weak branches, those

Hemlock and White Pine growing in the wild. Root pruning ahead of transplanting is certainly desirable and probably necessary to successfully transplant this Hemlock and White Pine.

They are root-pruned by thrusting a sharp-edged spade into the soil to its full depth, making a circle, in this case, about 9 inches from the trunk. The soil has been partly removed to show long thong-like roots that were cut off by the spade.

A year later fine feeding roots have developed on pruned roots of both trees —Hemlock on the left, Pine at the right. The Hemlock made these new roots close to the cut, but on the Pine they developed freely about 3 inches from the cut.

The Hemlock is dug up and stood on a square of burlap preparatory to tying it up and moving it to its new location. Soil has been scratched away from the circumference of the ball to show the compact root system which has resulted from root pruning one year previous.

Another Pine, not root-pruned a year earlier, after transplanting in the fall. New shoots are almost as long as those of the preceding year.

Now compare our old friend: root-pruned the previous year, it made shorter new shoots. New growth proportions of the two trees will be reversed next year.

Twelve years later the Hemlock is a sizable tree.

nearest the ground if a clear trunk is desired, those which are too close to a neighboring branch, any crossing branches, or those which spoil the symmetry of the subject. Trees with thong-like roots will need to have their tops pruned more severely than those with fibrous roots. The amount of the top growth to be cut off depends on the kind of tree and whether it naturally makes plenty of fibrous roots, such as *Euonymus,* and hence is easily transplanted, or whether the fibrous roots are sparse, as in Oak and Hickory. In general it is advisable to cut off about one third from the current shoots. Do not cut back the leader unless it is injured. If, after a few weeks of warm weather in the spring, the new shoots do not appear to be thrifty or if there is no sign of any growth, more cutting back is indicated.

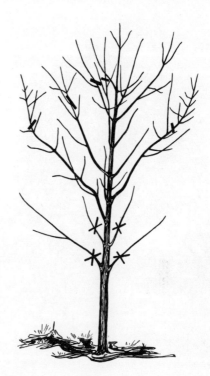

At transplanting time reduce branches for better symmetry and closer balance between the top and the roots. Cut at the trunk those marked X; others at the single black marks, each one close to the twig below it.

The branches marked X are being removed with pruning shears. Cuts are made as close as possible to the trunk. Sometimes it is more convenient with a tree this size to do the pruning before setting the plant in the hole.

The same tree twelve years after transplanting.

If the trees were growing in a nursery, close planting may have been deliberate so that the lowermost branches were killed by insufficient light. Such trees, when planted in the open, are vulnerable to sunscald unless the trunk is protected by wrapping it with burlap or with specially made crepe-paper strips, or the trunk and branches may be sprayed with an anti-transpirant such as Wilt-Pruf. These protectants should be left in place until the head has grown to such an extent that it provides ample shade for the trunk. If the tree has two leading shoots, the weaker should be removed; otherwise an undesirable V-shaped crotch may develop.

It is worthwhile to look over newly planted trees to see if there is any trouble that can be rectified by pruning, paying particular attention to the V-shaped crotches, which are a source of weakness. They are very likely to form on trees whose buds grow in pairs. Sugar Maple is particularly prone to these crotches. The remedy is to remove one of the arms of the V, or if this leaves too big a gap you might get by with shortening the weaker one. Also look for branches which cross and rub each other, and cut off the less desirable one.

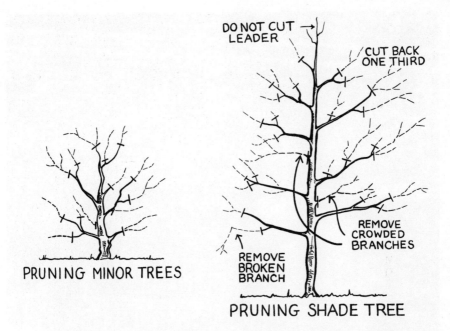

If the tree is supported by stakes or guy wires, they should receive attention. Possibly the tree can get along without them, in which case remove them. If they need to stay in place another year, be very careful to avoid having the ties so tight that there is danger of the trunk becoming strangled by its own growth.

Pruning Established Trees

This varies according to the object in view. If the tree is young and handsome, thinning out undesirable branches when the tree is dormant is the correct operation. Shorten any projecting branches that spoil the ideal outline, and when there are two branches which cross and rub each other, remove the less desirable one. If the tree is already large enough and the foliage is ample to cause dense shade, which for various reasons can be undesirable, the pruning should be done when the tree is fully leafed out in August. This is preferable to pruning it when it is dormant because it will slow down future growth and immediately let more light reach the ground beneath the tree. Usually this can be done by cutting

This *Morus alba* (Mulberry), because of its low branches, presented a problem when it came time to mow under it.

off fairly large limbs, making the cuts parallel with and close to the larger parent branch to avoid leaving stubs.

Because there are no growing parts on the stubs, there is no reason for sap to flow to their extremities; hence they die. The healing callus makes every effort to close the gap, but it is unable to do so. Meanwhile disease-causing organisms may get to work and decay may extend into the trunk or the large limb.

To do a good job of making a major wound, the cut should be made close to the trunk or to the branch from which it originates.

A close-up of the three cuts necessary to remove large branches.

The removal of a large branch usually requires three cuts, the first about a foot from the trunk, making an undercut by sawing upward until the saw binds. Then cut from above about 1 inch from the first cut to remove the branch. This will leave a stub which can be supported by one hand while it is being cut off parallel to the branch or trunk on which it grew. The reason for doing it this way is to avoid the possibility of the falling branch tearing off a large strip of bark from the trunk or parent branch. To promote quick healing, the wound ideally should be longer than it is wide. It may be desirable to make the wound in the shape of an ellipse by cutting into the bark above and below with a knife or chisel. If this is done the wound should be protected by covering it with a polythene plastic film or spraying it with an anti-transpirant preparation such as Wilt-Pruf. However, I would advise waiting for a time, before making the wound larger, to see if it will callus naturally.

There are differences of opinion among tree men concerning the desirability of protecting tree wounds made when pruning. The consensus seems to be that some protective substance should be applied, at least to the larger wounds—those 2 inches or more across. The dressing should inhibit the germination of spores of disease-causing organisms, prevent the checking (cracking) of the wood, and at the same time be non-injurious to the living tissue of the cambium. Shellac or a paint made of zinc oxide and raw linseed oil is conveniently obtainable and fairly satisfactory. Soot or lampblack may be mixed with the paint to make it less conspicuous. Also asphalt paints can be used with good results, or a paint especially formulated for tree wounds may be obtained from garden supply stores.

The first step—making the undercut.

The second step—cutting from above to remove the branch.

The third step—removing the stub.

The stub can now be held by the hand so that the cut can be completed without slivering the bark.

The completed job, but not satisfactory. The last cut should have been made much closer to the trunk.

Morus alba pendula (Teas' Weeping Mulberry). A freak of a freak is shown here. A strong upright shoot developed from the original, forming a more or less independent bush at top right. Often these are pruned by trimming all shoots the same distance from the ground, giving the effect of bangs or a Piccadilly fringe. It is difficult to advise how to best prune this weeping tree. I suppose a modification of the bangs idea is as good as any. This would mean cutting off some of the drooping shoots at different lengths in midsummer. It may be pruned in late winter by cutting out some of the old branches and shortening the shoots that grew the preceding year to about 6 inches or less.

It is obviously impossible for the healing callus to cover this entire stub.

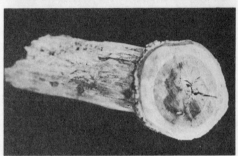

Decay-causing organisms had already made their way into the trunk from which this stub was cut. The stub should have been removed years earlier.

Roderick MacLeod is not holding a boar's head! It is the "C" cut shown in the close-up on page 87.

The opposite end of the stump, showing the wound left, is longer than it is wide, which is ideal for quick healing.

This *Cornus mas* (Cornelian Cherry) presents a job of work to be done. All those potential stubs should be cut off as close to the parent branch as possible. The spindling shoots which are not pulling their weight should be removed.

A stub is about to be removed.

A mature White Pine with numerous stubs which should be removed by cutting close to the trunk. The lowermost branch on the right also should be cut off.

Applying tree-wound paint.

Pruning Mature Trees

One of the reasons for pruning trees is to maintain and enhance their beauty. This does not necessarily require a great deal of pruning, because, ideally, the natural shape of the species should be retained as far as possible. This is not always feasible, because of spatial limitations which may require pruning to reduce the size of the tree or to slow down its growth. Many trees, especially coniferous evergreens, when grown as specimens in the open with no competition with other plants, normally are clothed with their branches from the ground up. This may not be desirable in a home landscape because the owner may want to utilize the ground beneath the tree either for planting shade-loving subjects or for an outdoor living area.

High-headed deciduous trees with a clear, clean trunk of at least 6 feet are desirable for shade and also for street planting. This may require the removal of branches below the head. In some cases it may be necessary to spread the pruning over several years because otherwise the trunk may suffer from sunscald.

Before you start to prune a tree it is advisable to study it thoroughly. There should be a reason for every cut that you make when pruning it. It is always safe to cut off any dead branches, also those which have been injured by wind. When two branches get together so that they cross and rub each other, one of them should be removed. If this cannot be done without spoiling the symmetry of the tree, the branches may be fastened together at the point where the bark is being abraded. This can be done by boring a hole through both stems and inserting a stove bolt of suitable length. The head and the nut should be countersunk. Treated in this way, the branches are held rigidly together and grafting will take place, which will remove the danger of spores of disease-causing organisms obtaining access to the tree through the wound. If the tree is not growing compactly, shortening the branch tips will force into growth buds that otherwise remain dormant. If there is an opening caused by the loss of a limb, it may be possible by pruning adjacent branches to direct the growth in that direction. If the pruning is done in such a way as to make a well-

Here is an example of making a high-headed tree the hard way. Sixteen branches were removed during eight years. While all the wounds have healed perfectly or are in the process of healing, it is not the best way to make a high-headed tree.

A better way to produce a high-headed tree. Ideally, work should be done with lopping shears while the tree is comparatively small.

This is a reminder that trimming a high-headed tree cannot be a rush job. The slender young man knew enough to spread the pruning of this tree over about five years, annually taking off the lowermost branch.

balanced tree while it is young, there will be but little need of pruning as it approaches maturity. V-shaped crotches usually are weak and whenever possible should be eliminated by cutting out the weaker of the branches. It is an impossibility to avoid all V-shaped crotches in trees such as Sugar Maple, and it may be desirable to cable two branches together and put a bolt through the tree toward the base of the crotch. (See picture of crotches on page 120.)

The time for pruning is late winter or very early spring. There are exceptions, however, with the trees which "bleed" profusely when they are cut toward the end of the dormant season. Among these "bleeders" are Sugar Maple, Birch, Walnut, Yellowwood, Beech, and Hornbeam, which should be pruned in September or October.

The tools required are lopping shears and a pole pruner or pole saw. The latter may be useless to shorten flexible branches because they wobble so freely that it is almost impossible to keep the saw in one cut. If you cannot do the job with these tools, it is advisable to get professional tree men to do the work.

When large mature trees are in question, pruning them is usually a job for a professional, even if his price does seem a bit steep. But it is better to pay it rather than a hospital bill, or for a funeral director, for you or a member of your family. It is as good as a circus to watch these tree men work on large trees. They are as agile as Tarzan and know exactly how to get around in the tree and the importance of using safety equipment. If, however, it is a case of removing a branch not too far from the ground, you may be able to do it yourself. Do not forget there is a right way and a wrong way of cutting off the branch. (See page 87.)

This is the less vigorous of two established Sweet Gum trees. The multiple leader needs attention. All leaders except one should be cut off. It must be done by means of a long-handled pruner, working from a ladder. An over-all shortening of terminal shoots will stimulate the growth of dormant buds and thus improve the appearance of the tree.

This more vigorous tree needs but little pruning beyond the removal of the crossing, rubbing branch.

A tree that lost its leader when it was about 12 feet high. It is doubtful whether the kink will ever be entirely overcome, but the tree can be immediately helped by cutting off the branch marked by arrow, remedying a bad crotch. At the same time, the clutter of weak shoots in the center should be cut off.

Here are two crossed and rubbing branches that are causing trouble. The one indicated by arrow should definitely be taken off. All branches below the horizontal lines could be removed for better landscape effect and function.

A close-up of the crossing branches shown in the preceding picture. One should be removed close to the trunk as indicated by arrow.

A variety of crotch formations—at the left the arrow indicates a weak crotch. At the right is a strong open crotch, the kind to be preserved.

Tarzan, indicated by arrow, is taking the top off piecemeal to avoid damage to the house.

The top has just been cut off. No attempt was made to avoid stripping the bark because the whole tree is being removed.

The trunk was left about 10 feet high and now serves as a support for a Trumpet Creeper.

Trees Sometimes Grow Too Large

There is nothing static about trees. At times they may grow too large in the positions they occupy. This is most often seen in plantings near the house or in foundation planting. Usually this trouble is caused by selecting wrong planting material. It is not unusual to see forest trees planted in situations where a height of 6 feet, usually less, is desirable. For a while these trees can be kept down by annual pruning, but ultimately the time will come when it is necessary to remove them and start all over again from scratch—this time choosing slow-growing varieties that do not rapidly grow out of bounds. Sometimes the problem can be solved after a fashion by pollarding—either annually or at intervals of two to five years. There is a good example of pollarded trees of *Platanus acerifolia* (London Plane, Sycamore, or Buttonwood) along a street near the railroad station at Kew Gardens, England. It is true that they look horrid for a time, but new growth quickly

One of the reasons for purchasing our present home was the numerous trees, which really made the place for us. As a matter of fact, there were too many. For example, the picture shows a group of trees located 50 feet northwest of the house, all growing in a space of 10 by 20 feet. The Buttonwood tree was taken out because it leaned toward the house and there was grave danger of its being blown down and landing on the roof. The three Ash trees were poorly shaped due to crowding, and in consequence they were marked for removal.

covers and eliminates the ugly look. I was not able to get back to take a summer picture of the London Planes at Kew, but I did take a picture of Lindens which had been similarly treated at Ely, Cambridgeshire. Actually the old Apple tree shown on page 107 represents a form of pollarding. Not every tree is adaptable to this kind of pruning. Among those that can take it are *Platanus* (London Plane), *Tilia* (Linden), and *Robinia pseudo-acacia* (Black Locust).

A close-up of the two Buttonwoods, showing the crowded
condition and partially rotted
knotholes, indicated by arrows.

The Buttonwood in the left foreground is the sole survivor of the clump.

This *Sophora japonica* (Chinese Scholar Tree) is in need of tree surgery. This specimen, growing in the Royal Botanic Gardens, Kew, England, is one of five plants that were introduced to cultivation in 1793. The two tree stumps to the right in the picture are props to hold up the two remaining branches of this patriarch. The cavity in the foreground should be cleaned out and treated with a disinfectant.

Pollarded Buttonwoods (*Platanus acerifolia*) used as street trees in the village of Kew, England.

Pollarded Lindens at Ely, England.

A mutilated street tree with apparently a dark future—but cheer up . . .

Just around the corner are some trees which had been similarly butchered several years previously. They do not look too bad.

An ancient Apple tree in need of rejuvenation. It was a major operation, involving cutting off branches up to 9 inches in diameter. This was done in the winter of 1947.

Rejuvenational Pruning

Old devitalized trees may sometimes have their vigor renewed by cutting off up to one third of their top growth when they are dormant. Good judgment is necessary to insure that enough is cut off to be of benefit but not so much that it results in the production of a thicket of sappy water sprouts. In general, the cuts should be made close to branches pointing in the direction in which you wish the trees to develop. The tree pictured is an ancient Apple, which, twelve years ago, looked as though it were on its way out. The trunk is 7 feet in circumference about 9 inches above the ground. Although it is not going to last forever, the treatment was decidedly worthwhile in this particular case.

Two years later the tree has made an astonishing recovery. While obviously living on borrowed time, it is making the most of it. With no further dying back, the top is round and full.

In 1952 the tree is furnished with strong, young, vigorous shoots.

In the spring of 1959, twelve years after the first pruning, the tree is still giving us a display of large, exquisitely fragrant flowers.

A Seckel Pear on its last legs, competing with brushwood and weeds.

With the aid of a mattock the weed shrubs and coarse perennials are grubbed out.

Pulling out the Poison Ivy.

Then the dying branches are cut off.

Roots are fertilized by making holes with a crowbar, 2 feet deep and 1½ to 2 feet apart, starting 3 feet from the trunk and outwards to 6 inches beyond the spread of the branches. A handful of 10-10-5 fertilizer is put into each hole.

A mulch of weeds and grass to the depth of 6 inches is put on the surface.

Flowering Trees

Specimen of *Prunus subhirtella* (Spring Cherry) grafted on top of an understock about 5 feet tall. This practice I do not like, because the skeleton does not look natural.

This one, to me, is much more beautiful, even though the branching is bizarre.

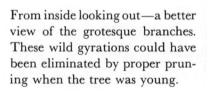

From inside looking out—a better view of the grotesque branches. These wild gyrations could have been eliminated by proper pruning when the tree was young.

Cherry Walk in the Brooklyn Botanic Garden. Apparently it is the nature of this variety of Japanese Flowering Cherry (Kwanzan) to originate its branches in a cluster. Doubtless manipulation by removing some of them when they were no more than a few inches long would have partially remedied this defect.

Prunus serrulata Kwanzan (Japanese Flowering Cherry) with fairly good scaffold branches.

Not so good as the preceding tree. Probably the splitting of the crotch can be prevented by pleaching—that is, by twisting together a couple of small branches, one from each main branch if such can be found. They will ultimately become grafted and provide support. Another way is to use wires fastened to screw eyes as described on page 226.

Here is a specimen of *Prunus incisa* (Mt. Fuji Cherry) which has never been pruned. As a consequence, it has just about everything wrong with it— branches that cross and abrade each other, bad crotches, and the center of the tree cluttered with small weak shoots.

And yet it was capable of producing a show of blooms like this.

Another count against it is that its branches overhang a walk so as to impede traffic.

Thinning out was done while the tree was in full leaf to avoid stimulating the growth of dormant buds, which are vulnerable to aphis attack.

Enough branches have been removed to gain the primary objective—that of making it possible to walk beneath it after a rain without danger of being doused with a shower of water.

Crotches

Eliminating a V-shaped crotch in a Flowering Dogwood. If a symmetrical tree with a single trunk is preferred, all of the top growth should be cut off except the strong-growing trunk to the right. Such pruning should be spread over three or four years.

Here is a Maple that has started splitting. A bolt with diamond-shaped washers has been installed and a cable has been put in (not visible here) to join the two trunks about midway between the crotch and the top of the tree.

Here is one of two trees growing in a nursery. This is the most desirable one because it has a definite leader.

This one can be improved by cutting off the branch at the arrow. Both trees should have some of their twiggy branches cut off where they are crowding their neighbors.

Suicidal Trees

Trees sometimes garrote themselves. When wayward roots grow around the trunk, or around other roots, expansion by subsequent growth often results in strangulation. Sometimes the tree is able to free itself from its own snare by breaking the offending root. I have such a one on my own place, but in this case the root was comparatively small and only a small part of the circumference of the trunk was involved, so that the vigor of the tree was not greatly impaired. Often, however, prompt remedial surgery is required when injury is first noticed.

The photographs show two examples of tree trunks (Sugar Maple) on which the despoiling work of girdling roots has started and which could result in the death of one, at least, if not corrected. Little damage has been done so far to one tree, and the condition can be remedied by cutting the entire exposed part of the girdling root and easing it out of the groove it has already made in one part of the trunk.

The situation was more serious for the other tree pictured. In this case a strong root was obstructing the flow of sap for more than half the circumference of the trunk. (The groove in the trunk made by the root is most clearly visible in the left half of the picture.) The result was the gradual dying of most of the branches on one side of the tree and a smooth, sickly-looking area of bark over the region where constriction started. In some places the growth of the trunk had partly enveloped the root, requiring careful work with chisel and mallet to remove the root without further injury to the trunk. The work was done by a good tree man and I had hoped that the tree would quickly improve, because it played an important part in shading my study. Later these hopes were not realized and the tree was in such bad shape it became necessary to cut it down.

In these two cases diagnosis was easy because the offending roots were in plain sight, having been exposed, I think, by erosion of the soil in times past. Sometimes, however, the condition develops below the surface. If the tree is not healthy and there is no other known cause—insect pests, fungus disease, gas, or a bad soil condition—girdling roots should be suspected; especially if, in addi-

Fortunately, in this case, the offending roots were clearly visible,
so the trouble could be remedied
by cutting them before too much
damage was done.

In the case of this tree, the injury
has extended too far. Perhaps it
would have been possible to delay
the hour of its demise by bridge
grafting.

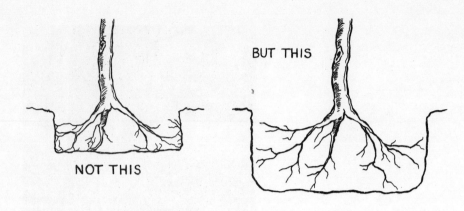

BUT THIS

NOT THIS

PRUNING SHADE TREE

When transplanting a tree it is essential to make the hole large enough to contain the roots without any bending.

tion to symptoms already mentioned, the trunk does not flare naturally at the base—page 123 (lower); in the top picture the "flare" has not yet been affected. If girdling roots are the cause of the trouble, carefully digging away the soil near the trunk should disclose them so that they can be dealt with.

Girdling roots may occur on naturally regenerated trees, but more often in those which have been transplanted. In the first case, the roots may have been diverted from their normal outward-spreading course by an obstruction in the soil which set it on the wrong tack. In transplanted trees, cramming the roots in a hole too small to allow for proper spreading may be a source of later trouble. It is well to look critically at the root system when transplanting a bare-root tree, and if any of the main roots look as though they are bent on mischief, cut them out if they can easily be spared; otherwise manipulate them and hold them in place by short stakes driven in below the soil level. By the time the stakes decay, the roots probably will be fixed on an innocuous course of travel.

CHAPTER X

Evergreen Trees and Shrubs

Narrow-Leaf Evergreens

This is the name applied to coniferous evergreens even though sometimes their leaves (as on *Podocarpus*) may be broader than those that are classed as broad-leaf evergreens, such as Heather and Heath.

Coniferous evergreens, with a few notable exceptions, such as *Thuja* (Arborvitae), *Tsuga* (Hemlock), *Juniperus* (Red Cedar), and *Taxus* (Yew), do not respond to severe pruning because they do not produce new adventitious shoots from old wood; therefore it is necessary to be circumspect in dealing with *Abies* (Fir), *Picea* (Spruce), and *Pinus* (Pine).

These never should be cut back into wood that is leafless. The best way to handle Pines is to shorten the "candles" when they have attained their full length before the needles are produced and/or cut the long terminal shoots back to the first or second whorl of branches. Ordinarily it is, or should be, unnecessary to prune a Pine except when a formal hedge is desired or to remove insect pests such as the pine-shoot weevil or in the case of foundation planting when they are getting so tall they obscure the view from the windows. These remarks also apply to *Abies* and *Picea*, substituting "young growth" for "candles."

In this connection I would like to remind you that it is important to start curbing those plants which are likely to exceed their bounds, *before* they reach the stage which is your limit for them. The reason for this is that a small portion of wood of the current season must be retained to maintain the plants in health. This brings a further reminder that only small- or slow-growing species should be used in the areas where low-growing plants are necessary, or that you should plant those that can take close shearing, such as Japanese and English Yew, Hemlock, and Arborvitae.

Pinus mugo (Swiss Mountain Pine) can be kept low by shortening the candles before the needles develop. This shows the stage at which they can be pinched back from one half to two thirds.

The branch to the left is one that was pinched back the year before. The one to the right, held by the hand, has not been pruned.

A close-up of a branch on which the candles were pinched back, showing the large number of shoots produced as the result of the pinching. If this is kept up for two or three years it makes a densely branched shrub with comparatively small needles.

The best time to prune coniferous evergreens in general is just before new shoots start in the spring, followed by shearing new growth when it has attained its full length or just before this, usually in June or early in July. Treated in this way, there will be additional new growth to mitigate the shorn look throughout the winter which occurs when pruning is done in September. Three prunings each year are permissible only when the plants are approaching the limit in size. In the case of Pines, after the main terminal shoots have been cut back, the "candles" of those remaining may be shortened by removing one half to three fourths of each candle.

To sum up, coniferous evergreens ordinarily are no problem except for the occasional cutting back of a shoot outstripping its neighbor; in the case of foundation planting, to prolong the time lapse before it becomes necessary to remove them; when a specimen of formal shape is required as an accent in a formal garden; when needed to form a hedge (see Chapter V); or for topiary (see Chapter VI).

Pinus strobus (White Pine) usually does not hold its leaves beyond three years. The terminal shoot can be removed just above the first whorl of branches or, if necessary, two years of growth could be cut off just above the second whorl.

This White Pine lost its leader several years ago. A lateral was chosen to take the lead, helped by tying it to a stake which was held vertical by tying it to the trunk of the tree.

Five years of growth of *Pinus syl-vestris* (Scots Pine), showing that it retains its needles two years longer than the White Pine. If pruning is being done to reduce the size, three or four years' growth may be cut off.

Picea abies (Norway Spruce), which holds its needles for six years (indicated by dots), can be pruned by cutting it back with hedge shears. If a more natural appearance is desired, or if it is necessary to reduce its size, it may be cut with pruning shears, taking care not to trespass by cutting needleless wood. In this case the cut should be made on the central stem just above the second marker from the top.

An upright Japanese Yew that has just been transplanted. Although this one would survive without reducing the top, it is just as well to shape it up by cutting off the shoots which have grown out beyond the general body.

Pruning completed.

Shortening wild shoots of Japanese Yew with secateurs.

Whenever it is possible to get a tree or shrub which will naturally serve your purpose with little or no pruning, it should be acquired. This dwarf Norway Spruce, which looks a little like a hamburger bun, is a form of *Picea abies* (*excelsa*). It is 4 feet across and less than 2 feet high and is at least thirty-five years old. The tall narrow specimen just behind it is a fastigiate form of the common Juniper—*Juniperus communis compressa*. It is admirable for any position where a slender upright specimen is needed. To the best of my knowledge, these two specimens have never been pruned.

Some evergreens, for example *Cedrus libani* (Cedar of Lebanon), not only are beautiful as seen from the outside in but also are of considerable interest from the inside looking out. The ruggedness of this specimen is comparable to that of White Oak. It can be improved by the removal of one of the crossing branches, indicated by the arrow.

Broad-Leaf Evergreen Trees and Shrubs

Broad-leaf evergreens seldom need extensive pruning except when they are used to provide formal accents and when they are used for hedges or edges, or when it is necessary to remove broken branches and those which have been injured as a result of a severe winter.

The number of broad-leaf evergreen trees that can endure sub-zero temperatures is definitely limited. The hardiest ones are

This *Sciadopitys verticillata* (Umbrella Pine) poses quite a problem! While this tree seems to be perfect when seen from a distance, close inspection shows that it consists of three trunks—the one to the right being of considerable size. Three courses are available: first, to leave it as is; second, to cut out the two superfluous trunks; third, to gradually suppress the redundant trunks by cutting the branches gradually, thus encouraging young shoots to fill in the gaps on the main trunk.

the *Ilex opaca* (American Holly) and, if you can find a source for it, *I. pedunculosa.*

Although there is, or was, a tree of *Magnolia grandiflora* (Bull Bay) growing in Brooklyn, New York, usually it is not reliably hardy in climates that are more severe than that of Washington, D.C. It is not too happy even on the northern part of the Pacific coast, where winter conditions are no problem but the lack of heat in summer might be a limiting factor. This can be overcome, to some extent, by growing it against a wall as is done in England, to take advantage of the extra heat radiated from the wall. *Magnolia virginiana* (Sweet Bay) is only semi-evergreen and takes a long time to grow to a sizable tree. Pruning these evergreen trees is usually restricted to the removal of unwanted branches or shortening "wild" shoots which grow out far beyond their neighbors.

Ilex (Holly)

Ilex aquifolium (English Holly), *I. opaca* (American Holly), *I. cornuta* (Chinese Holly), and *I. crenata* (Japanese Holly) are the most important of the evergreen hollies. The berries of all these are red except the last-named, which bears black fruits. South of Washington, D.C., *I. vomitoria* (Yaupon) and *I. cassine* (Dahoon) are used for hedges and topiary. Many examples may be seen in restored gardens at Williamsburg, Virginia.

Magnolia grandiflora (Bull Bay) espaliered against the wall, just to the right of the chimney, in the Oxford Botanic Garden, England.

Ilex opaca (American Holly) grown as a high-headed tree in the garden of the Governor's Palace at Williamsburg, Virginia. Doubtless it was helped in its early stages to get a clean trunk, but now it is not likely to need any further pruning.

I. aquifolium and *I. opaca* are grown under orchard conditions to provide Christmas greens and berries, the first-named on the Pacific coast and *I. opaca* in Florida. They are also used for hedge

Fruiting branch of *Ilex opaca* (American Holly) showing the short annual growth (indicated by dots). If the growth was vigorous—say, a foot or more in length —it would need shortening in June.

plants in regions where they are thoroughly winter-hardy. One clipping a year in summer just before the young shoots attain their full length is usually all that is needed. The annual cutting of the crop in December normally is all the pruning needed by those which are grown for Christmas greens.

I. crenata is very similar to Boxwood in its foliage characters. It can be distinguished easily, however, by its alternate leaves as compared with the opposite leaves of Boxwood. The straight species, *I. crenata,* may grow 20 feet tall in regions with mild winters. Some of the varieties, such as *helleri, convexa,* and *globosa,* are dwarf forms. The only pruning that any of these require is done in the spring, when the shoots injured by winter are cut off.

The Dahoon and the Yaupon need little pruning except when a formal effect is desired. They can be sheared as often as necessary during the growing season. The flowers of English Holly are produced on the growth of the preceding season; consequently pruning, if any, should consist of shortening the shoots of the current season before they attain their full length. The purpose of this is to avoid having the berries obscured by long vegetative shoots.

Ilex glabra (Inkberry) shows the gawky legginess of this species.

Heading back Inkberry to induce dormant buds to grow.

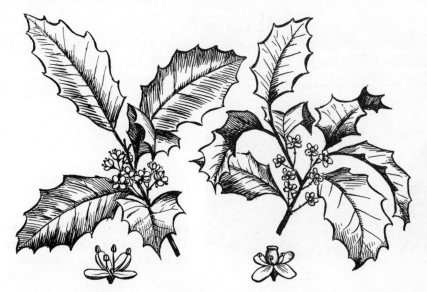

POLLEN-BEARING FLOWERS   "SEED-BEARING" FLOWERS

Male and female Holly—pollen-bearing at left and seed-bearing at right.

I. glabra (Inkberry), a semi-evergreen, tends to grow lax and gawky. It should be pruned by cutting back the shoots of the preceding year in the spring and the tips of the young growth again in June or July.

Perhaps a reminder is in order that, except for *I. burfordi*, a variety of the Chinese Holly, most hollies are dioecious—the staminate (male) and pistillate (female) flowers are produced on separate plants. Therefore it is essential to have at least one male plant for every 20–50 females to insure a good crop of berries. Other ways of solving this problem are to bud-graft the male plant on the female, or, if you know of a male plant from which you can cut branches when the flowers are open, place their butts in a bucket of water and put them in the vicinity of the tree that is to be pollinated. Honeybees and other insects will do the actual work.

Buxus sempervirens (Tree Boxwood). This has reached the stage where no further pruning is necessary.

Berberis (Barberry)

B. julianae (Wintergreen Barberry) is reputed to be the hardiest of the evergreen species. This and *B. triacanthophora* and *B. verruculosa* (Warty Barberry) need practically no pruning except to shorten shoots which may spoil their symmetry.

Buxus (Boxwood or Box)

Buxus sempervirens (Tree Boxwood) is capable of growing into a small tree up to 25 feet. *B. sempervirens suffruticosa* (Edging Boxwood) is the variety that is most commonly grown in America. This is the one which is a feature at Washington's home at Mount Vernon. In course of time it makes a handsome billowing mass up to about 40 inches high or more, but usually it is clipped to a formal hedge or edging. For edging it should be sheared in the spring and again in late August or early in September. Even with this regular pruning the plants will, in course of time, grow too large to serve as an edging. In such cases it is customary to dig up entire plants, if they are not more than 1 foot high, divide them, and reset them deep enough to provide the desired height, or shoots 6 inches or so long can be put in as cuttings late in August and set out the following spring. The remainder of the overgrown edge can be dug up and planted where it has a chance to develop.

Branch of Boxwood with dots to show annual growth. It can be pruned by cutting out the central shoot just above the lowermost dot or by making the cut just above the topmost dot or by an over-all shearing, or it can be left as is. The first-named method is used when it is necessary to restrict the size, the second when a more compact but still informal shape is required, and the third to make a compact formal shape. Best of all perhaps is no pruning at all.

Buxus sempervirens rotundifolia, about twelve years old, that has never been pruned.

The picture on page 39 (hedges) shows what happens when Boxwood used as an edging is neglected.

Calluna vulgaris (Heather)

There is only one species of the genus *Calluna,* but it is variable and there are numerous named varieties. They should be pruned, usually with hedge shears, by cutting off the faded spikes of bloom, in the spring before new growth starts.

Camellia (Camellia)

Unfortunately *Camellia* is not reliably hardy north of the Mason-Dixon Line. However, there are plenty of adventurous gardeners who don't mind taking a chance of growing them outdoors even in the Hudson River Valley. The two best-known kinds, apart from *Camellia thea* (Tea Plant), are *C. japonica* and *C. sasanqua.* The last-named blooms in late fall and early winter, while *japonica* blooms in late winter and early spring. Ordinarily there will be no need for pruning. If it does become necessary, it is comforting to know that it can be done without permanent injury even though it may involve cutting into the old wood. If necessary, they should be pruned immediately after blooming when the new growth is about to begin.

Daphne (Daphne)

Daphne odora, D. cneorum, and *D. burkwoodi* are the most important species of evergreen Daphne for outdoor gardeners. *D. burkwoodi* and *D. cneorum* are the hardiest. *D. odora marginata* is hardier than *odora,* but this is not reliably winter-hardy in regions north of Philadelphia. Little pruning is needed on any of these evergreen Daphnes except perhaps that the flower heads of *D. cneorum* may be sheared off as soon as the flowers are faded.

Erica (Heath)

Unlike its close relative *Calluna,* this genus contains more than 500 species. The winter-hardy kinds include *Erica carnea, E. ciliaris, E. cinerea,* and *E. vagans,* which can be pruned by shearing off their flowers when they fade. The tender kinds, which need the protection of a greenhouse in our climate, include *E. hyemalis, E. persoluta,* and *E. melanthera.* They can be pruned with hand pruning shears by cutting off the shoots that have borne flowers as soon as the flowers have faded. These Heaths are frequently obtainable from florist shops at Christmas and Easter time, where they are

Daphne odora marginata needs no pruning except the removal of faded flowers to prevent seeding.

Daphne cneorum, like its relative *D. odora,* needs little or no pruning—merely cut off the faded flower heads with hedge shears.

sometimes featured as "genuine Scots heather," which is naughty of the vendors because these species of *Erica* are really not Scotch at all. They are native in South Africa.

Although the Heaths and Heathers are included in the broad-leaf evergreens, actually their leaves are narrower than those of some of the conifers which are called narrow-leaf evergreens.

Euonymus (Spindle Tree)

Euonymus kiautschovica (*patens*) is semi-evergreen except in mild climates. The only pruning needed is the occasional removal of a branch which gets out of bounds.

E. fortunei is at least as hardy as the English Ivy, especially if it is grown on a north wall or where it is not exposed to winter sunshine.

E. f. carrierei is a shrubby kind which may require pruning to make it retain its shrubby form. The variety *vegetus* also can be trained as a shrub. It is more easily done if there is no support of any kind nearby to encourage it to climb. There is now available a series of shrublike cultivars produced by Corliss Brothers, Inc., of Gloucester, Massachusetts. They should be immensely valuable for foundation planting and for hedges. Among them are Emerald Cushion, a low spreading kind, and Emerald Pride, which in outline is like an old-fashioned beehive.

E. japonicus (Japanese Euonymus) is much less hardy than the *fortunei* group. It is a favorite in England as a hedge plant because it stands shearing quite well.

Hedera (Ivy)

Hedera helix (English Ivy) and its many varieties need annual pruning when they are grown as edging plants, as a hedge on a support of some kind, and where they are climbing on a wall of a house. The time to do this, in every case, is in the spring when new growth is beginning. Usually leaves as well as the shoots which developed the preceding year are cut off. This makes an unsightly mess for a few weeks but new growth quickly covers it. Paradoxically, hedge shears are used for trimming except in hedges, where hand shears are used to shorten projecting shoots.

The arborescent forms, which retain their character if the

Euonymus kiautschovica (*patens*), un-pruned, may develop scaffold branches which, separated from one another, look like individual small trees.

It can be pruned to emphasize this trait or the shoot tips may be cut off, which will result in a fairly close-knit shrub.

shoots are rooted from cuttings, need no pruning except for removal of the flower heads and wayward shoots which extend beyond the general outline, or when a reversion to the juvenile climbing form develops.

Euonymus fortunei Emerald Cushion and *E. f.* Emerald Pride show unpruned plants. If more compact specimens are needed, the shoot tips can be sheared in June or July. (See also "Hedges.")

Hedera helix (English Ivy) in need of pruning. It should be sheared as closely as possible in the spring, especially that growing on the steps, which is a hazard for anyone using them.

This picture of English Ivy was taken during the fall. The overwhelming growth was made since it was cut back the preceding spring. Most would look on this as too much of a good thing.

Hedera helix climbs a tree, in this case a Buttonwood. The danger here is, it may so weaken the tree that it is liable to be blown down because of the additional weight. To obviate this, the Ivy should be pruned back severely.

An arborescent form of English Ivy. This shrublike condition may be perpetuated by rooting cuttings.

It may revert to the climbing form as shown here. The shoot coming from the base is a reversion. Note the difference in growth habit and the shape of the leaves.

Hypericum (St.-John's-wort)

Hypericum moserianum (Goldflower) is a hybrid of *H. calycinum* and *H. patulum.* These are suitable ground covers in mild climates and can be used in the shade if it is not too dense. Pruning consists of cutting them back almost to the ground every spring.

Kalmia (Mountain Laurel)

Kalmia latifolia (Mountain Laurel) requires about the same kind of treatment given to Rhododendron. *K. angustifolia* (Sheep Laurel), sometimes called Lambkill, usually has a thin, open habit of growth. Pruning by shortening new shoots in the spring might overcome this defect.

Leucothoë (Fetter Bush)

Leucothoë catesbaei (Fetter Bush or Dog Hobble) is the best known and the hardiest of the evergreen species of *Leucothoë.* Usually no pruning is required, but if for any reason it is necessary, it is easy and consists merely of cutting off shoots which have borne the blossoms. This can be done any time after May when the flowers have faded.

Pieris (Andromeda)

There are two evergreen species of *Pieris* (*Andromeda*) commonly grown—*P. japonica* and *P. floribunda.* Like *Leucothoë,* they produce their flower buds in the fall, ready to open in April or May. It is seldom necessary to prune them. Any pruning should be restricted to the removal of wayward branches that may spoil the symmetry of the bushes.

Pyracantha (Firethorn)

Pyracantha coccinea and its variety *lalandi* are the hardiest of the Firethorns. Pruning of those grown to bush form consists of shortening "wild" shoots during the summer. When they are trained to grow against a wall (espaliered), they should be pruned after flowering by shortening all shoots except those which have borne flowers and those which are needed to extend the growth.

Rhododendron (Rhododendron) (see also *Azalea*)

One form of pruning which can be practiced on Rhododendrons annually to their advantage is the removal of flower clusters as soon as they have faded. This prevents the formation of seeds,

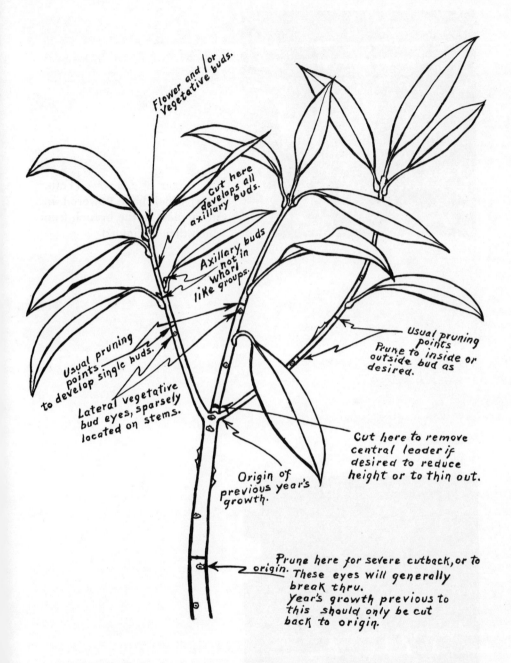

Showing method of pruning *Kalmia latifolia* (Mountain Laurel).

The shoots of *Leucothoë* (Fetter Bush) which have flowered are cut off close to the branch from which they originated.

A spent flowering shoot of *Leucothoë* which should be cut off at the point indicated by the arrow.

Mahonia aquifolium (Oregon Grape). This is a triple-promise shrub—flowers, fruit, and foliage color in the fall and winter. If they get too leggy they should be cut back, ½ to 1 foot, in the spring or they may be cut during the winter for Christmas decorations.

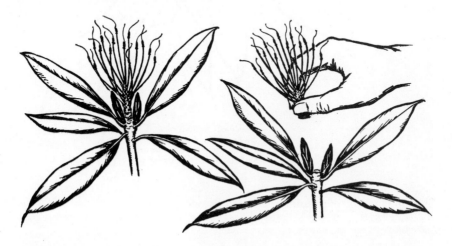

Method of removing faded cluster of flowers of Rhododendron to prevent seeding. The only precaution is to avoid injuring the growth buds.

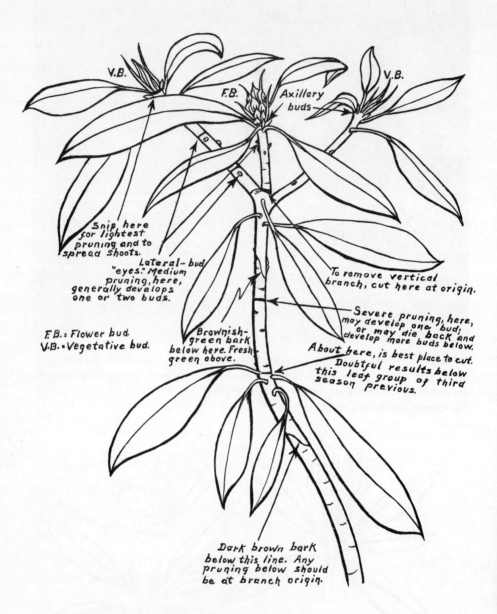

V.B.

F.B.   Axillary
        buds

V.B.

Snip here
for lightest
pruning and to
spread shoots.

Lateral-bud
"eyes." Medium
pruning, here,
generally develops
one or two buds.

To remove vertical
branch, cut here at origin.

Severe pruning, here,
may develop one bud;
or may die back and
develop more buds below.

F.B.= Flower bud.
V.B.= Vegetative bud.

Brownish-
green bark
below here. Fresh
green above.

About here, is best place to cut.
Doubtful results below
this leaf group of third
season previous.

Dark brown bark
below this line. Any
pruning below should
be at branch origin.

Showing method of pruning evergreen Rhododendron.

which is a drain on the plant's energy, especially in the case of newly set plants. No tools are necessary, as the cluster is easily removed by giving it a sideways downward pull with thumb and fingers. Obviously this is impractical when the bushes have attained a height and spread of more than 6 feet.

Pruning Rhododendrons in the sense of cutting back branches is to be avoided whenever possible. If, however, the branches need thinning to make the bush more shapely, or if the bush has grown too tall for its location, pruning is permissible because, as a rule, new shoots are freely produced even by old wood when the plant is cut back. Pruning should be done immediately after flowering, just before new growth starts in the spring. In the case of those species, for example *R. maximum*, which make new shoots before the flowers open, the flower display must be sacrificed to avoid having to cut off branches which already have started growth. Any pruning which demands severe cutting back should, if possible, be spread over a period of two or three years—cutting half or one third one year and the remainder after that.

The preceding remarks apply also to that group of evergreen Rhododendrons commonly known as Azalea. In addition, if a compact bush is desired, any new shoots which show a disposition to outstrip their neighbors may have their tips pinched off early in the summer.

Skimmia (Skimmia)

Skimmia japonica and its variety *reevesiana* are hardier than is generally believed. The last-named has survived about ten winters outdoors, planted among *Pachysandra* on the north side of our home about eighty miles north of New York City. Usually it does not need pruning, but if for any reason it is necessary, it should be done in the spring when the new growth is about to start.

Other tender or barely hardy broad-leaf evergreens include

Aucuba (Japan Laurel)

Aucuba japonica and its variety *variegata* (Gold-dust Tree) can be cut back severely in the spring if necessary to reduce its size or to improve its shape.

Laurus nobilis (Bay tree). Clipped specimens seen at Torquay, England. The trunk is abnormally short.

Laurus (Bay Tree)

Laurus nobilis, the true Laurel, better known perhaps as Bay Tree, is the tree which provided the material for the laurel wreaths bestowed on the winners of athletic contests by the ancient Greeks and Romans. Because of its amenability, it is commonly grown in tubs or large pots, sheared either to a hemispherical, pyramidal, or ball-like head on a clear trunk. These formal-shape laurels were formerly imported from Europe and were in great favor about fifty or sixty years ago, but with the coming of the Quarantine No. 37, which virtually prohibited the entry of them and similar plants, their popularity declined and now they are seldom seen. Difficulty in finding a place to store them for the winter and of obtaining help to bring them under cover in the fall and put them out in the following spring doubtless are factors in their loss of favor.

CHAPTER XI

Deciduous Shrubs

THE greater bulk of deciduous flowering shrubs blossom on short laterals, which come directly from shoots made the preceding year. Included among these are: *Philadelphus* (Mock Orange or Syringa), *Weigela* (*Diervilla*), *Kolkwitzia amabilis* (Beauty Bush), *Spiraea prunifolia* (Bridal Wreath), *S. vanhouttei* (Vanhoutte's Spirea), and *Buddleia alternifolia* (Garland Butterfly Bush). All the preceding are best pruned by removing annually a few of the oldest shoots by cutting them either to the ground line or to a strong one-year-old shoot, and by cutting back most of the shoots which bore flowers.

Berberis dictyophylla (Chalk-leaf Barberry) is unique in the way it retains its foliage. Even though it is deciduous, if cut in the fall it continues to hold its leaves indefinitely if the clippings are kept dry. Thinning out crowded branches is all the pruning needed. When this is done in the fall, the prunings can be used in dried arrangements.

Clematis. From the pruning standpoint there are two kinds of woody Clematis—those which bloom on shoots made during the current season and those which bloom on one-year-old wood. The first group includes practically all the large flowered hybrids, the *lanuginosa* type, the *jackmani* type and the *viticella* type. These bloom on summer shoots of new wood and therefore can be pruned when dormant, as severely as necessary, even so far as cutting them down to the ground. Among the most valued kinds which can be cut back severely are *C. texensis* (Scarlet Clematis), *C. paniculata* (Japanese Clematis), and *C. virginiana* (Virgin's-bower). The *florida* and *patens* types, including *C. montana* (Mountain Clematis), blossom on one-year-old wood. These are pruned with some sacrifice of bloom by thinning out the crowded growths before they start in the spring and by cutting off the immature tips of the shoots. An

Buddleia alternifolia (Garland Butterfly Bush). Pointing out vegetative shoot referred to in the next caption.

Removing many of the branches that have flowered by cutting them back to a strong, vegetative shoot. This serves a double purpose—that of keeping the bush youthful and eliminating the drab-looking branches which have finished flowering. Note the heap of prunings in the foreground at the right.

Clematis. The large-flowered Clematis are well represented by *C. lanuginosa candida,* shown here sharing a pillar with a Rose. Pruning in this case consists of cutting back severely, in the spring, the growth made the preceding year.

Various large-flowered hybrids belonging in the same group as the preceding and similarly pruned.

Clematis montana (Mountain Clematis) blossoms on shoots of the preceding year. Pruning is done by thinning out the flowering shoots either when they are in bloom or shortly thereafter.

alternative is to wait until they are through blooming before pruning. These are not so rugged as those in the first group and are not reliably hardy in regions more severe than those experienced on Long Island, New York.

If you are not sure of the group to which your plants belong, your best plan would be to assume that they are the kinds that bloom on the shoots of the preceding year. Then you will not be in the position of preventing them from blooming by cutting off all the growth of the preceding year.

Cytisus purgans, a relative of the Scotch Broom (*C. scoparius*). This specimen is dense enough, so it needs no pruning unless it begins to show legginess, in which case it will be given an over-all shortening immediately after bloom.

Cytisus praecox (Warminster Broom), *C. purgans,* and *C. scoparius* (Scotch Broom) have a tendency to grow leggy. Consequently, they should be pruned by clipping them as soon as the flowers have faded. They do not respond to hard pruning—*usually it is fatal to cut them back to the brown wood.* Although they are deciduous most of the functions of the leaves are taken over by the young green shoots hence for all garden purposes they are evergreen.

Deutzia, except for *D. gracilis,* which is compact, low-growing (about 4 feet), and seldom needs pruning, should be treated the same as *Philadelphus.*

Hydrangea

This genus contains both those which bloom on old wood and those which bloom on shoots developed during the growing season. The progenitor of the so-called "French" or Florists' Hydrangea is *H. macrophylla.* It is safer, with all of the many varieties of this species, to avoid cutting off any of the branches during the period of its dormancy, because, with the exception of one or two varieties, the buds which produce the blooms are either terminal or those near the tips of the canes. They should be pruned as soon as the flowers have faded by cutting out some of the weaker shoots, especially those which have blossomed. This is a good seashore shrub

Euonymous alatus compactus. This plant has grown too large, obscuring the view.

Cutting it back about 1 foot in July with pruning shears. While this did not accomplish the object, it did result in a more compact plant.

which is dubiously hardy inland at the latitude of Philadelphia. It can, however, be protected by covering the entire plant with earth, or by tying the shoots together and wrapping them with burlap, straw, or salt-meadow hay, which should enable them to withstand temperatures down to zero.

Its mate, which was not pruned during the growing season, is not nearly so compact.

Before growth started the following spring, we decided to be more drastic—cutting back into old wood with lopping shears and reducing the height of the bush by about 2 feet. This would have been fatal with some plants, such as the Brooms, which do not break from old wood.

Weak, twiggy growth is removed with pruning shears.

Forsythia intermedia (Golden Bells) is a classic example of a shrub which blossoms on shoots made the preceding year. Therefore they cannot be pruned during the dormant season without loss of blooms.

The same plant a year later. It needs considerable thinning out.

A start has been made, after the flowering season, by cutting out some of the older branches with lopping shears.

A well-placed Forsythia in need of pruning.

Many of the old canes have been removed, taking them from the base, using lopping shears or a narrow-blade saw. The prunings in the foreground at left can be used for forcing indoors if the job is done in the late winter.

Two years before this picture was taken, this shrub was a huge ungainly mass. It was cut almost to the ground. There is still some old wood which should be pruned out.

This is not the pleasantest job. Perhaps this is the reason we see so many shrubs in this state. Old wood is being removed with a pruning saw.

One way of dealing with Forsythia is that shown here. Each bush has a string around it—on the whole, giving rather a horrible effect.

Hydrangea quercifolia (Oak-leafed Hydrangea). The tips of most of the shoots were cut off in the spring. The only ones to produce flowers were the few left unpruned.

H. quercifolia (Oak-leafed Hydrangea) is trimmed in the same way as the preceding. The treatment accorded it is determined by the preferences of the owner, whether the flowers or the leaves are more important. If he wants flowers, he should try to keep the terminal buds from freezing, or if it is the leaves that are wanted, the shoots of the preceding year may be cut back in the spring, removing about one fourth of their tips.

H. petiolaris is the Climbing Hydrangea. This needs little or no pruning. All that is necessary is to cut back the flowering branches if their growth is so lush that there is danger of injury to the supporting tree or when it becomes so large that it may break away.

Schizophragma hydrangeoides (Hydrangea Vine). This is very similar to the preceding, differing in the sterile flowers, which have only one sepal, while those of *Hydrangea petiolaris* have three or four. Prune as indicated above.

Philadelphus (Mock Orange or Syringa)

These in general are pruned by annually cutting out a few of the older shoots and by cutting the flowering branches freely for decorating indoors. There is one species, *P. pubescens,* which is almost unbelievably gawky if left unpruned. This requires pinching out the tips of young shoots in order to make a well-branched and symmetrical shrub. As in the case of Forsythia, it is the two- and three-year-old branches which produce the best display of flowers. Consequently, some of them should be removed immediately after flowering to make room for the one- and two-year-olds.

Rhododendron calendulaceum (Flame Azalea) is one of the deciduous Rhododendrons popularly known as Azalea. This Azalea is believed by some to be the most beautiful of all native shrubs. It may be pruned while it is dormant with some loss of bloom. However, if it is vigorous, pruning can be left until the flowers are faded.

Syringa

Syringa vulgaris (Lilac) is commonly budded or grafted on *Ligustrum ovalifolium* (California Privet) or *L. vulgare* (Common Privet). When the graft has taken, the young plants are planted out in the field and deeply set with only the tip of the graft show-

Kolkwitzia amabilis (Beauty Bush). The pruning of Beauty Bush is essentially the same as *Buddleia alternifolia.*

Close-up of flowers. Cutting branches such as this to use indoors is a good way to prune this bush.

Improperly pruned by cutting back in the spring, before flowering, sacrificing the long graceful sprays of bloom shown in the preceding pictures.

Philadelphus. A *P. pubescens* which has been neglected for years, being pruned to bring it down to a symmetrical form. One gnarled, old branch has been removed. Another one is being removed with a pruning saw.

More old branches being removed.

All shoots in excess of 6 feet are cut back with pruning shears.

The following spring the vigorous tips are pinched out to promote branching and to keep it within bounds.

A *Philadelphus coronarius.* Some of the older shoots are taken out from the base, using lopping shears.

Old worn-out shoots are being cut off.

The old shoot has been cut off, leaving three strong young ones. A further cut is necessary to remove the stub.

The completed job.

Another way to prune *Philadelphus* is with hedge shears, giving it a crew cut, which may be all right if the surroundings are formal. This one is woefully out of place.

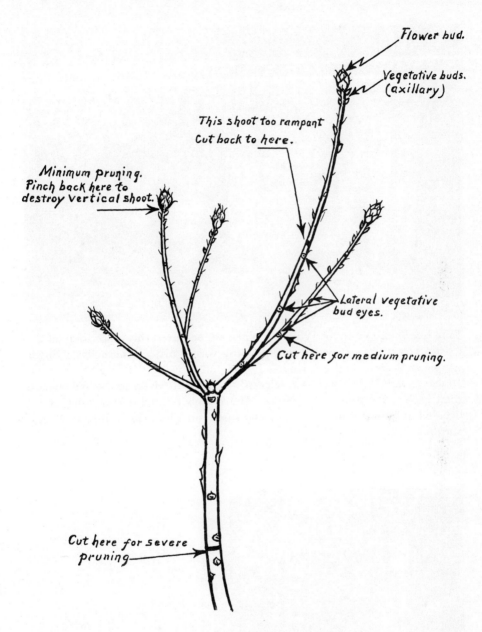

Flower bud.

Vegetative buds.
(axillary)

This shoot too rampant
Cut back to here.

Minimum pruning.
Pinch back here to
destroy vertical shoot.

Lateral vegetative
bud eyes.

Cut here for medium pruning.

Cut here for severe
pruning.

A dormant branch of Flame Azalea, showing method of pruning.

Salix babylonica (Weeping Willow). When we acquired this place some of the existing trees were crowded and pruning was in order. There was a Sugar Maple, a Willow, and a Carolina Poplar, all growing within a space about 10 feet square. The Maple was selected to be the survivor, so the Willow and the Carolina Poplar were cut down. The Willow refused to stay down, so we decided to humor it for a time, at any rate, and kept it pruned to serve as a shrub.

For a year or two it was possible to keep this Willow within bounds as a very graceful shrub. It eventually grew too large for the space allotted it, reaching 10 to 15 feet in height and more in width.

As it looked just before pruning started in the spring.

The head was brought down by cutting off large branches to strong laterals.

Reducing still more by shortening the main stems.

Still too broad, so some of the main stems are removed with an ax.

Mission accomplished.

ing. When these plants are dug up for their first transplanting, the privet understock, if it is not already dead, can be cut away leaving only the lilac roots. Saddle grafting is the method used because the base of the scion is placed in such a way that it readily calluses and ultimately produces its own roots.

Wisteria (Wisteria)

There is a widespread but erroneous belief that *Wisteria* has to be grafted to enable it to bloom. Failure to bloom may depend in part on the inherent nature of the individual, but chiefly, I think, on the environment and how it is pruned and treated. Seedlings and cuttings should bloom in two or three years if they are planted

Spiraea prunifolia plena (Double-flowered Bridal Wreath) seldom needs pruning, but when its shoots become spindling, like those on the upper left, it is a good plan to get rid of a few of the older branches by cutting them off at the base. This should be done when the flowers begin to fade.

in full sun and in soil not overly rich in nitrogen and pruned during July by shortening the shoots of the current season. These shoots should be cut to within about 6 inches of the branch from which they originate. Leave only those needed to extend the growth of the plant. It seems as though they are more likely to bloom when only a limited space is available on the trellis on which they can climb. Thus those which are trained to make standard plants or to bush form are likely to bloom earlier because of the severe pruning during the growing season.

Wisteria floribunda (Japanese Wisteria) may in some varieties, such as *W. f. macrobotrys,* have racemes of flowers 4 or 5 feet long, but *W. sinensis* (Chinese Wisteria) with racemes 6 to 12 inches in length is more popular. Perhaps the reason for this is because the Chinese Wisteria opens all its flowers at the same time, whereas the Japanese forms open gradually from base to apex.

Old shrubs which are making poor growth may be given new lease on life if they are cut back almost to the ground. It should be recognized, however, that such pruning is to be avoided as much as possible. Ideally, the treatment for shrubs which tend to become decrepit with age is to maintain constant juvenility by the removal, annually if necessary, of old worn-out wood. If this is done it greatly lessens the danger of upsetting the balance between roots

Syringa vulgaris (Lilac). Lilacs should be groomed. Their flower buds are produced at the ends of strong shoots. Weak non-flowering shoots should be cut off and suckers removed at the base (both shown in gray, left above) to allow plenty of room for present and future flowering shoots to develop properly. Drawing at right shows a well-groomed plant during blossoming.

To help maintain the symmetry of the bush and promote strong growth, crowded shoots may be pruned off close to another strong shoot. The crossline indicates such an operation.

A too tall, poorly shaped Lilac may be cut back, as indicated by the cross-lines, to renovate it and induce vigorous new growth.

An overgrown Lilac.

Most of these suckers must be cut off.

All the old branches are cut down to varying heights of less than 6 feet with a pruning saw. Wispy branches are being cut off with hand shears.

After twelve years of neglect we are back where we started.

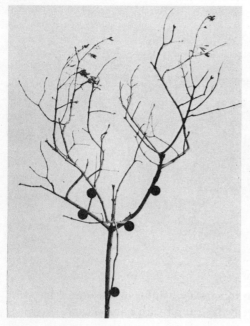

A branch with mostly weak, twiggy growth. It should be cut back severely, as indicated by the dots.

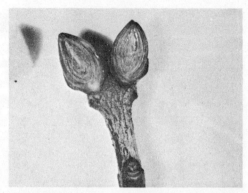

Twig taken from the preceding. Terminal bud cut through longitudinally, to show there are no blossoms.

This branch is much more vigorous than the one on page 184; consequently, pruning is less severe. Cut back as shown by dots.

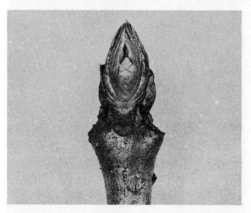

Longitudinal section through terminal bud from the branch in the preceding, showing flower cluster.

This is the common white Lilac, which tends to grow tall. The suckers have been removed each year to keep it to a single trunk.

Shortening lanky growth with lopping shears.

Removing weak, twiggy growth with hand shears.

Pruning finished.

The only pruning needed here is the removal at the ground line of the branch straying off to the right.

A young plant of *Weigela rosea* Vanicek which really does not need any pruning, but cutting one or two sprays of flowers is permissible.

Proper pruning may help *Wisteria* to bloom. For, popular favorite though it is, it often proves a problem child. Above left, harsh dormant pruning tends chiefly to encourage rampant vegetative growth suggested in gray. If pruning is delayed until after the normal flowering period has passed and then restricted to cutting back overvigorous vegetative growth, shown at right, also in gray, the tendency will be to stimulate production of flower buds which may bloom the next season.

Wisteria trained to bush form by summer pruning of new shoots.

and tops. Thus it may be desirable to spread corrective pruning over several years, or cut about half of the wood marked for removal during the winter and then check the overvigorous growth by removing the remainder during the following summer. Done in this way, it obviates the loss of blossoms for one year, possibly two or three. Among the shrubs that are amenable to this treatment are *Philadelphus* (Mock Orange), *Deutzia, Syringa* (Lilac), *Weigela,* and *Forsythia.*

Shrubs which produce their blossoms on wood one year old or older cannot be extensively pruned when they are dormant without reducing the number of flowers produced in the spring. This

An ancient *Wisteria* which was planted to climb on a building constructed in 1761. In the year 1861 the building was taken down, and to save the *Wisteria* an iron structure was provided.

A *Wisteria* in bloom. A little later the plant will produce its trailing new shoots, which must be cut back to within 6 inches of their point of origin.

does not necessarily mean that pruning this class in winter when they are dormant is absolutely prohibited. Lilacs can be pruned without much loss of bloom the following season if the parts removed are restricted to suckers and weak, twiggy, and spindling branches. Occasionally branches bearing flower buds may be deliberately sacrificed so that those remaining will have a better chance to develop. *Forsythia* (Golden Bells), *Jasminum nudiflorum* (Yellow Jasmine), and *Chaenomeles* (Japanese Flowering Quince) can be pruned late in winter and the prunings brought indoors to be placed in water, where they will open their flowers in advance of those left on the bush. As a general practice, however, it is well

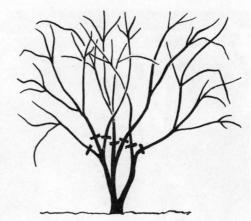

Buddleia davidi (Butterfly Bush) and certain other "die-back" shrubs can be pruned back severely prior to their making new growth.

to prune these early-blooming shrubs which flower on old wood, immediately after they have finished blossoming. Pruning should consist of the removal of worn-out wood and correcting irregularities of growth. Comparatively late bloomers from old wood such as *Kolkwitzia* (Beauty Bush) and *Buddleia alternifolia* (Garland Butterfly Bush) can be pruned by cutting off many of the branches which have produced flowers. Cutting the flowering branches for indoor use serves, in part, the same purpose as regular pruning and in some cases, for example Lilac, it is an important means of preventing the plants from increasing too rapidly in height.

Cut-Back and Die-Back Shrubs

There are some shrubs the tops of which are not entirely winter-hardy in locations where the temperatures may fall to 10 degrees or lower. Examples are *Abelia grandiflora, Buddleia davidi* (Butterfly Bush) and its varieties, *Vitex* (Chaste Tree), *Callicarpa japonica* (Beauty Berry), *Caryopteris incana* (Bluebeard), of which Blue Mist and Heavenly Blue are outstanding varieties, and some varieties of *Rosa* (Rose). They are pruned in the spring, cutting them back to the living wood. In severe climates it may be desirable to mulch these shrubs early in the winter with straw or something similar to protect the roots.

Caryopteris incana (Bluebeard). The sprawling plant in the foreground was not cut back in the spring. It would have made a better-looking plant had this been done.

There are some which can be treated as cut-back shrubs even though the tops may not suffer as a result of the winter. Among them are *Hydrangea arborescens grandiflora* (Hills of Snow) and *Spiraea bumalda* Anthony Waterer. These may be pruned by cutting them almost to the ground line in the spring or the flowers may be cut off as soon as they begin to fade.

Ailanthus altissima (Tree of Heaven) and *Paulownia tomentosa* (Empress Tree) are sometimes grown to a single stem which each year is cut to the ground before growth starts in the spring.

Treated in this way, they make strong shoots with leaves which are extraordinarily large. These are used to obtain an exotic effect where subtropical bedding is practiced.

Hibiscus syriacus (Rose of Sharon or Shrub Althea) and *Tamarix pentandra* (Summer Tamarisk), which blossom on shoots of the current season, can be pruned before growth starts in the spring. Shrubs which may be similarly pruned are *Hydrangea paniculata grandiflora* (Peegee Hydrangea), Hybrid Perpetual, Hybrid Tea, and other Roses.

Hydrangea paniculata grandiflora has been widely condemned by garden writers, including this one, but it has its good points, especially if it is pruned correctly. This means cutting back, about one third, the shoots of the preceding year. Many gardeners and landscape architects object to this Hydrangea, saying that the foliage is coarse and the flower heads are too flamboyant. Perhaps this is true when they are pruned back in the spring so that each stem can produce only one or two growth shoots, but when they are pruned moderately the plant looks entirely different. When it is left without pruning, more especially in the variety *praecox,* the plant is really quite handsome.

H. arborescens grandiflora (Hills of Snow). This is commonly pruned by cutting it down almost to the ground line in the spring. It probably is the best way to treat it.

Those shrubs which are grown for the color of their twigs in winter, such as Red-osier Dogwood, should be pruned before growth starts to promote the production of an ample supply of one-year-old twigs. This can be done by cutting them severely in the spring when they are dormant, followed up by pinching out the tips of the shoots when they are about 10 or 15 inches long. The Pussy Willow belongs in this same group so far as technique of pruning is concerned. If the desideratum is to have "pussies" produced on long whiplike growths, pruning should be severe just before leaf growth starts. Those who prefer the pussies displayed on short, twiggy growth should refrain from excessive pruning by limiting it to shortening the shoots produced the preceding year about one third.

Hibiscus syriacus (Rose of Sharon or Shrub Althea) unpruned is a pleasant-looking shrub compared with the following.

This has been cut back annually for a number of years.

The result of pruning by thinning out some of the crowded branches. The natural shape of the bush is maintained.

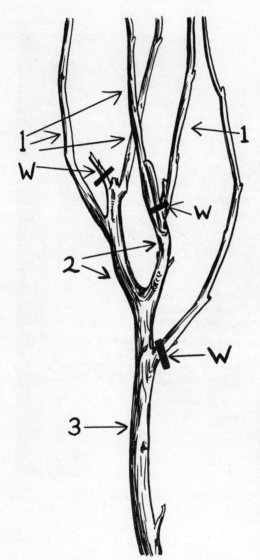

Hibiscus syriacus (Rose of Sharon or Shrub Althea) produces its flowers on growth made the current year and it should thus be pruned—as and if necessary—before new growth starts. The branch above shows, by numerals, the age of its growth in years. Leggy one-year growth is all that needs be kept in bounds. *W* indicates weak growth to be pruned.

One defect as a result of severe pruning of *Hydrangea paniculata grandiflora* is that the flowering panicles are so heavy that the branches are not strong enough to hold them erect.

A comparatively small unpruned bush of Peegee Hydrangea.

A laissez-faire policy is not always a success. A strong shoot which started from the base of the bush the previous year made five or six flowering shoots (those above the lady's hand) the current season. It should have been pruned by pinching out the tip of the extra-vigorous shoot when it was about 18 inches long.

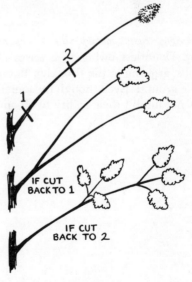

Hydrangea paniculata grandiflora flowers on the current year's long shoots. If cut back to the point marked *1,* two sturdy blooming shoots will develop; if cut back only to *2,* a larger number of smaller blooms will result.

Vitex agnus-castus macrophylla, V. negundo, and *Clerodendrum trichotomum*—left to right. Doubtless owing to a series of mild winters, this group of die-back shrubs, growing in the Brooklyn Botanic Garden, has not recently been killed to the ground. Even though (as sometimes happens) they are killed back, this does not inhibit their ability to bloom during the current season.

CHAPTER XII

Annuals and Herbaceous Perennials

ALTHOUGH the importance of pruning herbaceous plants is not so great as it is for woody plants, there are some that are benefited by being pruned.

Aster novae-angliae (New England Aster). The New England varieties of Michaelmas Daisies, after they have attained a height of about 2 feet, should be cut back, removing the upper 6 inches. It is difficult to explain why this should result in improvement—perhaps it is because it upsets the domestic arrangements of the aphids which attack these plants.

A. novi-belgi (New York Aster) should be pruned by removing all but the three strongest shoots in each clump when they are about the size shown in the picture of Phlox. (See page 216.)

Chrysanthemum. When you have bought or raised single-stemmed, rooted cuttings and want them to develop as bushes, the tips should be pinched out with thumbnail and forefinger to stimulate buds into growth below the pinch. The resulting branches, in turn, should have their tips pinched out when they have grown to a length of about 6 inches. Continue doing so until July. Pinching is unnecessary when you are growing so-called "Cushion Mums" and "Azaleamums," which are naturally bushy and do not need any encouragement to branch.

On the other hand, you may want to grow the large-flowered kinds which have come to be associated with the football season and Thanksgiving. These, contrary to the Garden Chrysanthemums, need to be disbranched and restricted to one, two, or three shoots per plant. But you must have the right variety. There is no point, for example, in growing small-flowered Button Chrysanthemums to a single stem and allowing only one flower to develop. Among the right varieties are: Chrysolora, Early Frost, Good News,

Rooted cuttings of Chrysanthemum, showing laterals resulting from the first pinching.

Golden Wave, Indianola, Mrs. H. E. Kidder, Rose Perfection, Silver Sheen, Smith's Superlative, and Stately White. Most of them are comparatively late bloomers and may be caught by frost. Usually these are grown in pots so they can be brought under cover if frost threatens. Each shoot should have a separate stake to which it is tied. Any shoots which appear in the axils of the leaves should be removed as soon as they are large enough to pinch out.

The selection of the kind of flower bud is important. The first one to appear is called the "first crown bud." With most varieties this does not usually give a good bloom, so it is removed. Then the second crown bud appears, which may be *the* one. If, however, this one is passed up, you have another chance in the terminal bud. The time for "taking" (choosing) these buds has been worked out by florists so that the beginner does not have to worry so much about which bud will be the best for him to keep. It is told in the catalogues of the dealers who specialize in Chrysanthemums.

Dahlia variabilis (Dahlia). The stock for planting may consist of a fleshy tuberous root which is cut from the clump (which grew the preceding year, was dug up in the fall, and kept in a cool, dry cellar over the winter) to include an eye (growth bud), or may be "green plants" obtained by rooting cuttings. When the shoot has grown to the height of 12 to 18 inches, the tip is pinched out with

The first crown bud.

The gardener's choice. The second crown bud (arrow) can be selected, or if that means that the completed bloom will be ready too soon, the shoot on the left will be selected by cutting at the positions marked.

A Chrysanthemum with typical cluster of buds.

The way the plant looks after being disbudded.

A Chrysanthemum crown bud
with normal laterals.

The same plant when thoroughly
disbranched and disbudded.

a thumbnail and finger. Usually the pinch is enough to obtain a sufficiency of strong branches, but if only two to four are obtained, further pinching may be necessary to obtain the required number, which will be six or more. The treatment from now on will be concerned with disbudding, which consists of removing all flower buds except one to each branch. Usually the one that is left will be the terminal bud. Treated in this way, the energy of the plant will be concentrated in the few buds that are left, and admirable flowers with long stalks suitable for exhibition will be produced.

If you are concerned mainly with flowers for home consumption or for garden display, you can forget about pinching and disbudding except for the removal of faded flowers. The small-flowered kinds — Miniatures, Pompons, and Balls — need no disbudding.

Delphinium. When the flowers of Delphinium have faded, cut them off to prevent them from going on to produce seed. Then, a few days or a few weeks later, when the leaves look ratty, cut all stalks down to the ground. Treated in this way, there is a possibility of getting another crop of flowers before frost.

Dianthus plumarius (Cottage Pink) and similar low-growing carpeting plants should be sheared either with grass or hedge shears to remove the flower stalks as soon as the flowers are faded. Others in this group are: *Viola cornuta* (Tufted Pansy); *Veronica,* dwarf and dwarfish varieties such as *V. teucrium, V. spicata,* and *V. incana; Lobularia (Alyssum) maritima* and *Alyssum saxatile* (Golden Tuft); *Armeria maritima* (Thrift); *Iberis sempervirens* (Perennial Candytuft); and others.

Iris. Tall-bearded Irises are pruned when they are transplanted by cutting the leaves back one half to two thirds. This can be done with ordinary scissors or one-hand grass shears. The only other pruning that may be necessary at times is to cut out, with a knife, portions of the rhizomes when they have been attacked by iris borers.

Phlox carolina (Summer-flowering Phlox), the early-blooming kind, and *P. paniculata* (Summer Perennial Phlox), of which there are innumerable named varieties, should be pruned early in the

The terminal shoot is being removed from Dahlia. This may delay the onset of flowers for a week or two but more will be out at one time.

The first pinch in this case produced only two laterals.

spring when the shoots are about 2 inches high by removing all but three of the strongest shoots. This is assuming that the individual plants are spaced about 1 foot apart. It is essential to cut off the panicles of faded blooms to prevent self-seeding. The seedlings, which revert to the ancestral forms, are more vigorous than the named varieties and consequently crowd out the original planting.

Two laterals resulting from the first pinch have, in turn, been pinched and each has produced two laterals. This will probably be enough if the owner has the show bench in mind.

Pinched three times but not disbranched, six to nine strong shoots have been developed.

Two fully open flowers can be cut for use indoors. Most of the remaining flower buds will open at the same time and make a good garden show.

Dahlia pinched above second pair of leaves to induce branching.

The same Dahlia disbranched and disbudded.

Cut off all the fading flower stalks of Delphinium.

A few days or a few weeks later they are ready to be cut to the ground.

New shoots originating from the rootstock may produce a second crop of bloom if an early frost does not get them.

Hedge shears used for clipping faded flower stems of Dianthus. This makes a neater clump and, more important, prevents seed formation, thus conserving the plant's energy and preventing mongrel seedlings.

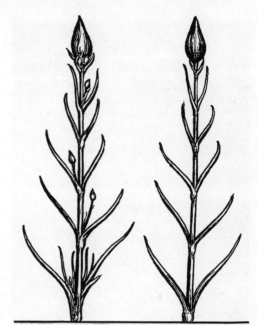

Dianthus caryophyllus (Carnation or Clove Pink). Varieties of this are commonly grown as cut flowers in greenhouses. They are usually disbudded, leaving only one flower to each shoot.

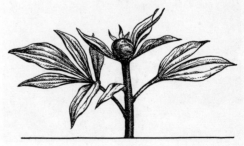

Paeonia albiflora (Peony). The garden forms of Peony should be disbudded by pinching out all but the terminal bud on each shoot. It is true that some of the lateral buds will open if they are left on, but the flowers are disappointing compared with those from the terminal buds and come as an anticlimax.

Thinning out superfluous shoots of Phlox, leaving no more than three to each clump.

The hard woody stems which grew the preceding year should be cut off with secateurs at or just below the ground line.

Cutting off faded flower panicles of Phlox to prevent the production of seeds. This serves a double purpose, that of conserving the plant's energy and eliminating the danger of self-sown seed.

CHAPTER XIII

Pruning House Plants

ONE does not usually think of pruning in connection with house plants, but there are some cases when it becomes eminently desirable. The principles are the same as for ordinary outdoor pruning. The cut should be made just above the leaf which has in its axil a bud pointed in the direction you want the plant to develop. Pruning can be done to advantage in September when the plants are dug up from their outdoor stations preparatory to spending the winter indoors. *Abutilon hybridum* (Flowering Maple) and *Hibiscus rosa-sinensis* (China Rose) can be pruned by cutting back the shoots of the current season about one half, or they can be pruned to advantage after repotting them in late winter (see Fuchsia).

Chrysanthemum hortorum (Garden Chrysanthemum). Pinch out the tips of shoots whenever they attain a length of 6 inches, until mid-July. When 1-, 2-, or 3-stem plants are desired, they are disbranched as soon as the required number of main shoots has been produced by removing all side shoots when they are large enough to handle. Larger flowers are produced by disbudding, removing all but the strongest buds from each shoot. See also Chrysanthemum under "Herbaceous Perennials."

Citrus Limonia (Ponderosa Lemon), *C. paradisi* (Grapefruit), *C. sinensis* (Sweet Orange), *C. taitensis* (Otaheite Orange). The only Citruses commonly offered by dealers in house plants are Ponderosa Lemon and Otaheite Orange. The Grapefruit and Sweet Orange usually are started from seeds for house plants. Pruning consists of the removal of weak, twiggy growth.

Coleus (Painted Nettle) can be grown either as a single-stemmed plant or a branching one. Your own preference will decide which. If you plump for the first-named method, it will require taking

Citrus paradisi (Grapefruit) raised from seed. No pruning is necessary at this time. In the future it will probably be desirable to cut the twiggy portion (arrow) to make room for the strong shoot which has taken the lead.

out axillary shoots, as in the case of *Saintpaulia;* otherwise just let nature take its course, with occasional help from you in the matter of pinching out shoot tips to prevent blossoming whenever necessary. The flowers of *Coleus* are not attractive except for a few species such as *C. thyrsoideus.*

Euphorbia pulcherrima (Poinsettia). The old plants should be cut back to within about 6 inches of the pot in April or May, repotted, and put outdoors for the summer. Cuttings may be taken from the cut-back plants during July and early August. This last method is preferable because it results in plants of moderate size. No further pruning is necessary.

Fuchsia. Resting plants should be brought into light and warmth about the end of January. When the buds start growing, repot the plants and cut back to the strongest shoots. If a bushy plant is required, the tips of the new shoots should be pinched out when they have made six or eight pairs of leaves.

Gardenia. If the plant is getting too large, prune it back one third before you set it outdoors in the spring. When the new shoots are about 6 inches long, pinch off the tips to promote branching. Do not pinch them after July.

Euphorbia pulcherrima (Poinsettia). At left, plant pruned in May by cutting all canes to within 3 or 4 inches of the soil. At right, as plant should appear three or four months later.

At Christmas time.

Saintpaulia ionantha (African Violet). Side shoot about to be removed with pointed pencil. Learn to distinguish flower buds from the tiny shoot buds. Flower buds look like a small knot made up of one or more flower buds. The leaf buds are leafier.

Tibouchina semidecandra (Princess Tree). Blossoms from the tips of the young shoots. As soon as the flowers are faded they should be cut off as indicated by the arrow.

Hedera helix. Although English Ivy, *Hedera helix,* can be used as a house plant, it is better to choose one of the "self-branching" mutations, such as Pittsburgh, Hahn's Self-branching, Manda's Crested, Pittsburgh Variegated, or Shamrock. Pruning can be done by pinching out the tips of the shoots to make the plants more compact. There is a non-climbing variety, *H. h. erecta,* which tends toward a sprawling habit. It may require removal of some of the sprawly parts if you wish a compact plant. Rarely, it may be possible to obtain small plants of the arborescent form of English Ivy. The pruning of this requires the removal of the flowering panicles and any shoots which have reverted to the juvenile climbing habit.

Nephthytis afzeli, Scindapsus aureus (Ivy Arum), *S. pictus argyraeus, Philodendron cordatum* (Heart-leaf Philodendron), and similar climbing Aroids should be pruned by pinching out the tips of the shoots as soon as they are about 8 inches long. If you have large plants growing on a support, such as a tree-fern trunk, a slab with bark on it, or a stout stick with moss wired on it, wait until they reach the top of the support.

When other trailing plants such as *Cissus antarctica* (Kangaroo Vine), *C. rhombifolia* (Grape Ivy), *Ipomoea batatas* (Sweet Potato), and *Boussingaultia baselloides* (Madeira Vine) have reached the limits of their supports, the tips of the shoots should be pinched out to stimulate the growth of buds which otherwise would stay dormant.

Pelargonium domesticum (Lady Washington Geranium). Shorten strong shoots in August or September and remove all weak ones. *P. hortorum* (House, Fish, or Zonal Geranium), when dug up in the fall, should have the top growth cut back at least one half. If they show any tendency to make lanky shoots, pinch off the tips and give them more light.

Rhododendron indicum (Greenhouse Azalea) may be pruned immediately after flowering, but do not cut them back any more than is absolutely necessary to make a shapely bush. During the summer pinch out the tips of shoots which are outstripping their neighbors.

Saintpaulia ionantha (African Violet). The chief pruning to be done on African Violets is that which is necessary to maintain a single-crown plant. It is best accomplished by removing the side shoots when they are barely visible, pushing them out with the aid of a pointed stick or pencil. Other pruning that may be considered desirable is the occasional removal of a wayward leaf.

Tibouchina semidecandra (Princess Tree, Glory Bush, or Spider Flower), a plant of many aliases, which has been called by botanists *Pleroma tibouchina, P. macranthum, P. splendens,* and also *Lasiandra semidecandra,* has the good trait of blooming while it is still young. This can be pruned by cutting off the terminal shoots when the flowers have faded.

Hoya carnosa (Wax Plant) needs but little pruning. Merely pinch out the tips of young shoots which are exceeding their bounds. Do not cut off the spurs (stubby growths) from which the flowers are produced.

CHAPTER XIV

Fruit

FRUITS which are most likely to be valuable in a temperate zone garden may be divided into pome fruits (Apple, Pear, and Quince), stone fruits (Peach, Apricot, Cherry, and Plum), Grape and small fruits (Raspberry, Blackberry, Blueberry, Currant, and Gooseberry).

Pruning is directed to the production and maintenance of a tree which permits the sun to reach the innermost branches. This facilitates harvesting the crop and, by opening up the tree to the air and sun, lessens the danger of attacks by fungus diseases. It makes it easier to secure better coverage by sprays and dusts against insects and fungi. This is done by thinning out crowded branches. On the other hand, it may sometimes be necessary to induce lateral branching by cutting off the tips of the larger polelike branches.

Obviously something is wrong here. Carpenter ants finished the job about a year after this picture was taken.

The new shoots, no more than 3 or 4 inches long, are indicative that all is not well.

So as it was desired to keep this Apple tree, we decided that the best way to do so would be to bud-graft it. The bud has started to grow and the understock is being pruned back.

Ten years later it was a healthy young tree. It was pruned by rabbits and deer, which accounts for the low branching habit. It can, however, be put in shape by pruning—cutting off some of the lower branches and thinning out the top.

An Apple tree with two weak crotches.
This can be corrected by cutting off the
branch at the right, or perhaps a better
method would be to fasten the three
branches together by wires fastened to
screw eyes inserted at the points indicated.

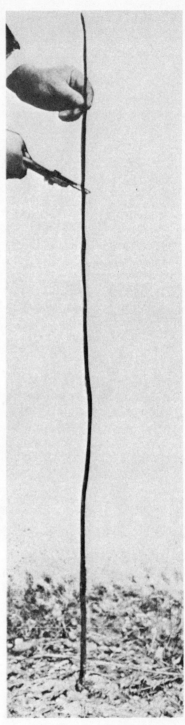

A one-year-old Apple tree is being pruned
by heading it back immediately after
planting.

Apple after one year in the orchard before pruning.

The same tree after pruning,
showing the evenly distributed
scaffold branches.

A four-year-old Apple tree before pruning. Pruning was primarily a thinning out of sucker growth from the trunk and scaffold limbs. A very little thinning in the top of the tree was all that was required.

The four-year-old Apple after pruning.

This Apple is trained to an open center. It, probably, would be advisable to head back some of the long polelike branches by cutting off a foot or so of the tips.

This one was developed under the modified-leader system. Little pruning is needed beyond the cutting back of crossing branches.

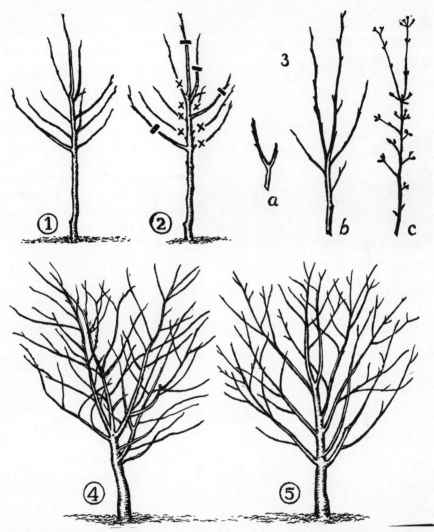

(1) A two-year-old nursery-grown tree, as received and planted. (2) The same tree after being pruned. The *X* signs indicate the branches removed entirely. (3) Effects of cutting back compared with thinning. (a) Twig severely cut back. (b) Growth from cut-back twig is all vegetative (no flowers). (c) Growth from tree with thinning pruning only; nice balance of twig growth and flowering spurs is clearly evidenced. (4) Neglect of early training results in poor framework. A Stayman Apple about six years old with objectionable three-leader, polelike growths and bad crotch. To correct now means a high head. (5) Early training results in good form. Stayman Apple about six years old; good spacing of scaffold branches, though they appear somewhat whorled. Central leader still present. Note development of secondary branches.

Bosc Pear before pruning. While this was planted on a dwarfing understock, it has probably made its own roots, judging from its vigorous growth.

It was pruned too severely, which resulted in the production of numerous water sprouts, up to 5 feet long.

Most of the water sprouts were removed.

Pome Fruits

Apple. One- or two-year-old trees are usually planted which may be single-stem whips or branched. They should be cut back to about 4 feet. If the one-year-old plant already has branches, it may be possible to select some of them for the "scaffold" branches. These will be the main branches and, ideally, should be distributed equally around the main trunk and from 6 to 9 inches apart. Perhaps there will be insufficient suitable branches at the end of the first growing season, but the following year the growth will probably be such that enough branches will be available from which the remainder of the scaffold branches may be selected. Very little additional pruning will be needed during the next five or six years or until the flowers are formed. One thing to watch out for, though, is a possible development of undesirable crotches.

Pear needs very much the same kind of pruning as Apple except that, because of its tendency to grow upright, the cuts when made should always be to an outward-pointing lateral or bud, or to one which when it grows will fill a gap in the branches.

Quince usually is trained in bush form to insure against the danger of losing the entire plant if attacked by borers. Pruning consists of removal of superfluous suckers and thinning out the top whenever the branches become too crowded.

A well-branched one-year-old Peach tree, as received from the nursery unpruned. It was headed back to a height of 40 inches and the lateral shoots cut back to a single bud.

Stone Fruits

Peach, Nectarine, Apricot. When one-year-old Peach trees are planted the usual method of pruning is to cut all lateral shoots to a single bud and shorten the leader to 24 inches. The following year the laterals should be shortened to induce branching. Subsequent pruning consists of cutting out some of the crowded branches to open up the center of the tree to air and to sunshine. Flowers are produced on the shoots of the preceding year. Cutting back some of these shoots is good practice, as this is one method of thinning the fruit. Nectarine is a fuzzless Peach and requires the same treatment. Apricot pruning is essentially the same as that of Peach except that fruits are produced on spurs as well as on the wood of the preceding year. Consequently, the spur growths are not cut off so long as they continue to bear.

Plum. There are three principal groups of Plums—European, Japanese, and hybrids. Plums are quite likely to over-bear, which may cause breakage, especially when named varieties are planted;

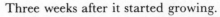

Three weeks after it started growing.

This one was cut back to 18 inches when it was planted. The scaffold branches are too close for best results.

After the branches for the framework of the top had been selected and the others cut off close to the trunk.

A four-year-old Peach tree before pruning.

Same tree after pruning. The pruning given at this age consists principally of thinning out inside shoots.

consequently, the modified central leader system of training is preferred (see Apple). Scaffold branches are selected as soon as possible. Meanwhile the leading shoot should be maintained until a sufficient number of scaffold branches are functioning or until the tree has reached the required height, when it is cut back to the first strong lateral. Weak shoots which are not pulling their weight should be removed annually. Pruning to remove shoots infected with black-knot fungus is commonly necessary.

Cherry. Sweet Cherries and the Japanese Flowering Cherries tend toward an upright habit of growth, which can be maintained by pruning. Some of the varieties seem to bunch their shoots (see picture on page 114) instead of producing them at 6-inch intervals, which is a desideratum. I am inclined to think that it is a regular habit with some types of edible Cherries and the Japanese Flowering Cherries to produce the main branches within a comparatively small compass on the trunk.

Preventing the trees from producing their main branches in clusters can be done to best advantage when they are young. This is accomplished by pinching out most of the branches with thumb and finger when they are no more than an inch or two long. Once the scaffold branches are established little or no further pruning is needed beyond cutting out dead wood. Occasionally it may be necessary to cut back a branch that is developing too rapidly and to thin out crowded branches.

Sour Cherries have a bushy habit of growth. The scaffold branches should be selected as soon as possible. The lowermost branch should start at least 20 inches above the ground line. The leader is maintained until the tree has almost attained the desired height. Then it is headed back to the first strong lateral branch. From time to time, when other branches take the lead, they also are cut back to the nearest lateral and it may be desirable to cut the weaker of two crossing branches.

Grapes

The bearing habit of Grape vines is such that pruning annually is really necessary. The fruit is produced on shoots which originate from canes which grew the preceding year.

Prunus cerasus (Sour Cherry) needs very little pruning. Thinning crowded branches is sometimes desirable to enable pickers to get around in the tree. This one can be improved by cutting off unproductive twiggy shoots from the center of the tree.

GLOSSARY OF TERMS

Trunk is the chief stem of the vine.

Arms are the parts of the vine which are two or more years old, excluding the trunk.

Canes are one-year-old shoots. *Shoots* grow from these and bear fruit. The following year they are called *canes*.

Head is the area on the trunk from which *arms* and *canes* are produced.

Spur is a *cane* which has been cut back to one or two buds.

There are several types of Grapes grown for their fruits, including *Vitis vinifera* (European Grape), *V. labrusca* (Fox Grape), and *V. rotundifolia* (Muscadine Grape).

Grapes may be grown on a trellis, pergola, or arbor, as part of a pleached allée, or they may be trained to make a canopy over a patio to enable the owner and his friends to sit in the shade of the vines. Commercial vineyardists use a trellis consisting of posts, 8 or 9 feet long, 6 to 8 inches in diameter at the butts, set about 20 feet apart, standing about 6 feet above the ground. These are put 2 feet 6 inches or 3 feet deep. Remove bark from the posts and treat them with copper naphthenate (Cuprinol) or creosote to retard decay. The posts are connected by two galvanized wires, No. 9 or No. 10, stretched tightly (use a wire stretcher, obtainable from horticultural-sundries men), one 30 to 36 inches from the ground and the other 30 inches above the first wire. The end posts must be braced firmly, preferably by the method indicated by the sketch. The wire is put once around an end post and fastened securely. It is run along the windward side of the posts, which are set approximately 20 feet apart, and when stretched and fastened at the other end it is stapled to the intervening posts. These intermediate posts can be sharpened and driven into the soil. If the soil is so stony that they can't be driven into it, you will have to use a posthole digger. The staples are driven in so that there is room for the wire to slide whenever it is necessary to tighten it. It should be attended to annually when frost gets out of the ground in the spring. At this time the posts, which probably

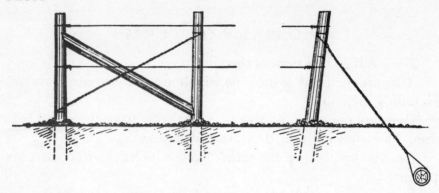

Two methods of supporting the end posts of a wire trellis. The one on the left is usually preferred because it does not have any wires extending beyond the post. The one on the right uses a "deadman," consisting of a log of decay-resistant wood about 2 feet by 6 inches with a No. 9 wire wound once around its midriff, or a rock of similar size and shape can be used. A hole 2 feet by 2½ feet deep is dug and the log or rock buried in it.

have been partially heaved from the ground as a result of freezing and thawing, can be driven in with a maul.

The above method is primarily utilitarian. Grapes can be used to furnish arbors or they may be espaliered. The vines should be trained fanwise on one or both sides of the structure alternating with vines grown to a single trunk. Pruning of the fan-trained sections consists of cutting back old canes that have produced fruits and replacing them with new ones started from spurs left for that purpose the preceding year. The single trunk, when it reaches the top of the arbor, is cut back to form a head, from which a number of canes will be produced. These are trained fanwise to cover the top of the arbor and provide fruiting shoots. Or it can be continued as a single trunk which is spur-pruned.

Pruning depends in part on the variety and in part on the system of training. The *vinifera* types for the most part are grown in California and are commonly pruned in such a way that the plant is self-supporting, the large head containing many spurs; or they can be trained using a modification of the following system.

In the varieties of *V. labrusca*, of which the best known is Concord, the favorite system of training is the Kniffin, either the four-cane Kniffin or the two-cane Umbrella Kniffin. Start with a one-year-old vine rooted from a cutting the preceding year. The plants are set in the soil 8 or 10 feet apart as early as possible in the spring and each one is cut back to a single cane, which in its turn is cut back to leave only two or three buds. During the first season the plants are allowed to sprawl along the ground at will. The second year the vine is again cut back, leaving only the strongest cane, which is cut to leave only two buds. The third year the strongest cane should be long enough to reach the top wire of the trellis, where it is tied (this will be the trunk). Two of the next-strongest canes are tied left and right to the lower wire and shortened. During the following growing season two strong shoots from the tip of the trunk are trained along the top wire, left and right; some fruit may be expected from the canes on the lower wires. The fourth-year pruning will be that accorded the mature vine. Four canes will be selected to carry the fruit, one right, one left, on each of the arms. These should be cut back to leave from 25 to 60 buds, depending on the vigor of the vine. In addition, four canes are cut to spurs as near as possible to the trunk.

Umbrella Kniffin. In this system of training the trunk is carried up to the top wire and two strong canes are selected, one right and one left, plus four cut-back spurs close to the head of the vine. The canes are placed over the top wire and carried down to the lowermost, where it is tied. If sufficiently vigorous, it may be taken up to the top wire again and tied.

The practice of weighing the prunings of one-year-old wood to determine the number of buds to leave is on the increase in New York State. For an example of how the practice works, see the table below, taken from *Cornell Extension Bulletin 805,* New York State College of Agriculture, Ithaca, New York.

WEIGHT OF CANE PRUNINGS	NUMBER OF BUDS TO LEAVE FOR FRUITING		
	CONCORD AND DELAWARE	FREDONIA	CATAWBA
Less than 1 pound	Less than 30	Less than 40	Less than 25
1 pound	30	40	25
2 pounds	40	50	35
3 pounds	50	60	45
4 pounds	60	70	55
More than 4 pounds	60+	70+	55+

A Concord vine as it may look in the fall or winter before its annual pruning.

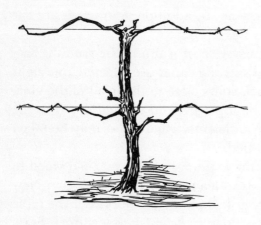

The same vine after being pruned according to the Kniffin system. The support wires are 30 and 60 inches above ground level.

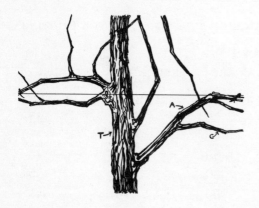

Detail of the drawing of the Concord vine before pruning: *T*—trunk; *A*—arm, two-year wood; *C*—cane, one-year wood.

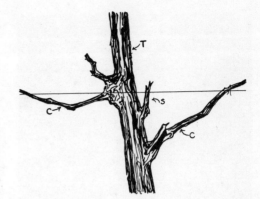

Detail of the drawing of the Concord vine after pruning: *C*—renewal cane, tied to wire; *S*—spur, one-year cane cut back to two buds; *T*—trunk.

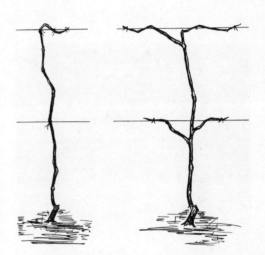

One-year and two-year vines after pruning. On the latter, five buds on each top cane, four on lower.

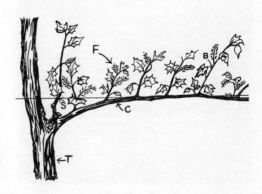

In bloom: *T*—trunk; *B*—shoot, current season; *C*—cane; *F*—flower cluster; *S*—spur with strong shoot for the following year's cane.

This shows the habit of growth of a vine that has been neglected too long. Notice the length of the stem held by the workman.

The vines were disentangled and a sufficiency of comparatively young growth was selected, cut back severely, and tied to the trellis.

Here is part of the crop produced the second year after pruning.

Sometimes it is necessary to rejuvenate a neglected vineyard. We had such a one on our place. The vines were disentangled and laid out on the ground to see plainly the kind of material we had to deal with. The first step was to get rid of the oldest, gnarly trunks. Then enough comparatively young material was cut back severely and tied to the trellis, remembering that the shoots grown from canes that were produced the preceding year are the ones that bear fruit. The following fall we got enough grapes to make a few quarts of juice. The next year we had plenty of grapes for eating and juice. We had to call on friends to help us use up the crop from a row fifty yards long.

Muscadine Grape is valuable in the Deep South. It is not hardy in the North. The fruit is produced in "bunches" containing only two or three grapes. They can be harvested by shaking the vines and picking up the grapes from the ground. Pruning is similar to that of the Concord types except that, usually, more buds may be left on the canes. In home gardens they are commonly grown on an arbor which provides shade as well as fruit.

Small Fruits

Blackberry when planted in the fall should be cut back to 6 inches. Blackberries need plenty of room, so set them 3 feet apart in rows 8 feet apart. During the second summer cut off at the ground line those canes which have fruited and cut back the remaining canes about one third. The following spring cut back the laterals about one third and the thin, spindling shoots to the ground line.

Boysenberry, Dewberry, Loganberry, and *Youngberry* are trailing Blackberries which are not winter-hardy in the northeastern states. The fruit-bearing canes are tied to a trellis, but those which are to bear the following year are allowed to trail along the ground. When fruit has been gathered the canes which have produced it are cut away and those which were lying along the ground are tied in their place.

Blueberry. The High-bush Blueberry (*Viburnum corymbosum*), so far as I know, is the only kind that is extensively cultivated commercially. Often the named varieties have a tendency toward over-

A fruiting branch of Blackberry.

In this Blueberry the tips of the
strongest shoots could be pinched
out and the crowded branches
thinned to let more light into the
center of the bush.

A Red Raspberry being pruned with a spade to remove super-fluous runners.

bearing. This is not good, because coupled with it is the fact that the berries sometimes do not ripen properly. Furthermore, over-bearing one year may result in lack of berries the following year. The remedy is to cut off weak, twiggy shoots and to remove one or two of the oldest branches annually and possibly cut off some of the weaker of the fruit-bearing shoots. This is a case, as always, of using your own perceptions in deciding how much pruning is desirable, because some varieties are more prone to over-bearing. Also they may behave differently in bearing in different environments.

Red Raspberries are planted 5 by 5 feet apart, or when they are grown in a solid row, 3 feet apart in rows 7 feet apart. In the first system the stakes are set at planting time in the spring, while in the row system plants are set 3 feet apart and are tied to wires which are stretched along the row. The pruning consists of removing, in the summer, the canes which have fruited. This will make room for the new shoots to grow which will provide the fruiting canes for the following year. In the spring the canes are cut back about one fourth before growth starts, and any weak or crowded shoots are cut off at the ground line. Red Raspberries have a suckering habit which requires the use of a spade to keep them within bounds. The row should not be allowed to exceed 15 inches in width with the canes no closer together than 6 inches.

Red Raspberry in the spring when the buds are beginning to grow. The canes made the preceding year are cut back about one third.

The pruning is finished and compost for a top dressing is applied.

A Red Raspberry, at fruiting stage, that has been grown according to the hill system.

A Red Raspberry grown in a row supported by horizontal wires.

The canes from which the berries
have been gathered are cut off at
the base. Either lopping shears or
a berry hook can be used.

This shows the kind of branch
removed by summer pruning
after the fruit has been gathered.

Showing the business end of a
berry hook. It is essential that
this be very sharp; otherwise it
may pull the plants up by the
roots.

A fruiting branch of Raspberry
(September) early in the fall.

A Blackcap Raspberry showing
what happens if it is left too long
before pruning. The canes of the
preceding year have arched over,
so that the tips have come in contact with the ground, where, if
not prevented, they will take root.

Purple Raspberry showing good growth habit. Pruning is similar to that of Blackcap Raspberry.

Blackcap Raspberry. Unlike the Red Raspberry, these do not produce any suckers. The new canes should be tipped when they are about 2 or 3 feet high, which causes them to branch. The lateral branches should be cut back the following spring to about 9 inches.

Purple Raspberry, a tremendously strong grower, is similar in growth habits to the Blackcap, but the top growth is not so hardy as that of either the Blackcap or Red Raspberry. Because of this strong growth, it is not adapted to small gardens. In this same category are the Trailing Blackberries, which are even more vigorous.

Currant. Red, White, and Black Currants act as alternate hosts to the destructive white-pine blister rust. Black Currants are seldom grown in this country, partly because they serve as the favorite

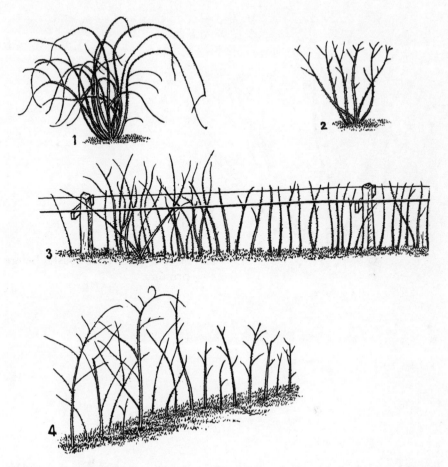

Numbers 1 and 2 show a Blackcap Raspberry before and after pruning to eliminate weak growth and long, arching canes. Number 3 demonstrates one way of handling Red Raspberries between parallel wire supports. The canes at the right have been pruned. Number 4 is a bush Blackberry row, pruned at the right.

alternate host to the blister rust and partly because the fruit does not appeal to American palates. Pruning of Red and White Currants should be directed toward the maintenance of five or six branches not more than three or four years old. This is done in the spring by cutting out at the ground line, annually, branches four or more years old. When they are planted in rich soil it may be necessary to shorten or pinch out the tips of Red and White Currants about midsummer. Do not pinch out the tips of the Black Currant.

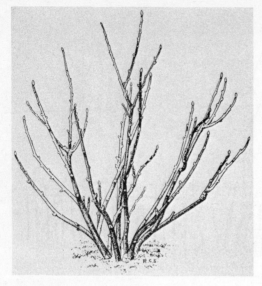

A Red Currant bush before pruning.

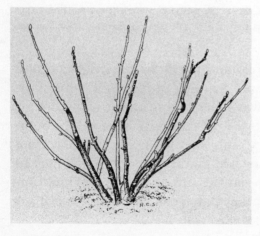

The same bush after pruning.

Gooseberry in need of pruning.

The lower branches have been removed and the remainder has been thinned out. Because of the vicious thorns, this thinning is necessary to facilitate picking.

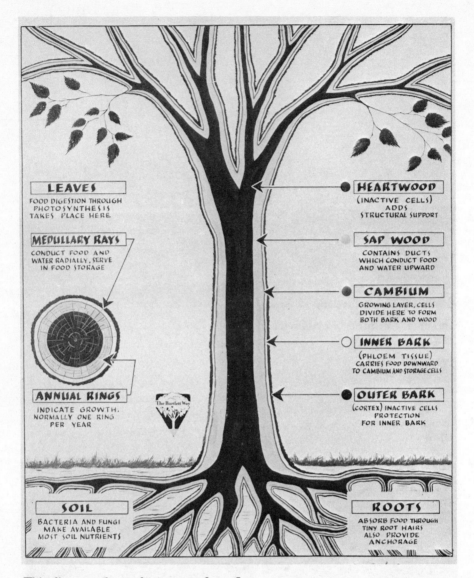

This diagram shows the course of sap flow.

Gooseberries are also on the "black list," because they, too, are alternate hosts to the white-pine blister rust. Pruning involves cutting out branches four or more years old and those which grow so low that the fruit may be spattered with mud during heavy rains.

Fig is fairly hardy with winter protection in climates no more severe than that of Long Island, New York. Figs are produced in the axils of the leaves of one-year-old shoots. Fruits sometimes are developed toward the close of the year, and if they are protected from the winter, they may come through to ripen their fruit early the following year. Pruning in cold areas is designed to develop a shrublike plant rather than a treelike one, so, when plants are starting in the spring, tips are cut back, which stimulates adventitious buds to grow. The following year the tips of shoots are again cut off to further promote young shoots. In succeeding years crowded branches may be thinned out. Attempting to grow figs in severe climates is questionable. The amount of work required to protect them over the winter is out of proportion to the value of the crop. Success is more certain when the bushes are espaliered against a wall which radiates heat and thus helps to ripen the young shoots. (See page 264.)

Ringing

This form of pruning is not commonly done nowadays. It consists of the removal, in the spring, of a cylinder of bark from a shoot of the preceding season. The depth of the cylinder varies from ⅒ to 1/16 inch. It depends for its effectiveness upon the fact that, in dicotyledonous plants, the course of the moisture absorbed by the roots from the soil with minerals dissolved in it is *upward* through the outer layer of the sapwood to the leaves. There it is combined with the help of chlorophyll, sunshine, and carbon dioxide to form starch and sugar, which are carried *downward* through the phloem (inner bark). Ringing thus puts a roadblock on the translocation of elaborated food toward the roots. It is done sometimes to bring about early fruiting and sometimes to obtain material for making cuttings which because of the concentration of food are more likely to root. It is believed by some that, applied to Grapes, it increases the sugar contained in the berries and improves the flavor of the crop. This practice should be done with great care to avoid the possibility of permanent injury to the plant. There are some who prefer to use half cylinders by making the cuts about 2 inches apart on opposite sides of the branch.

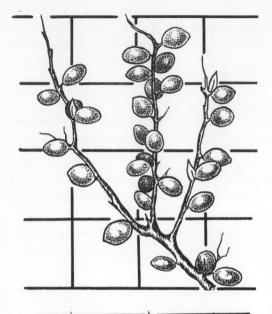

Unthinned Peach branch lies against a 6-inch grid. The crop will be far too heavy.

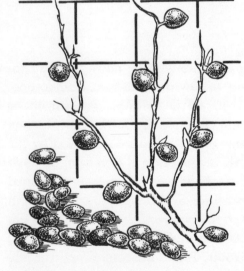

Here is the same branch thinned to an average of 6 inches apart—a safe interval.

Thinning Fruit

Thinning fruit is a form of pruning which is important to amateurs as well as commercial growers. In a good year when there are no late frosts to change the picture and it is not so rainy that the bees are kept home, there are usually more fruits set than the tree can take care of. Nature ordinarily takes a hand in this

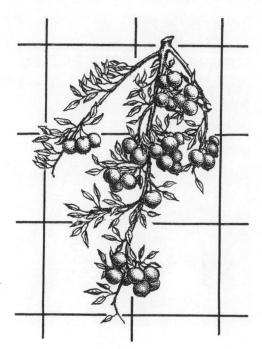

Typical overloaded branch of Apple before thinning. Squares are 12 inches along all sides.

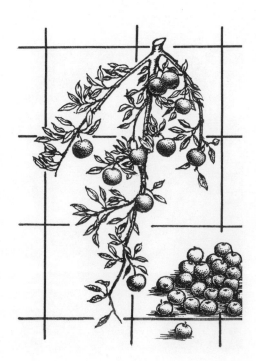

The same branch thinned to average 8-inch intervals. Pile shows fruit removed.

Espaliered Nectarines growing in a greenhouse. The shoots which produced fruit have been cut off and the new year-old shoots are tied in place.

A close-up of the tying.

Nectarine in blossom, trained to fan shape on a temporary support.

case by what is known as the "June drop"; however, this may not be sufficient to remedy the situation. Thinning may be done by chemicals applied at blossom time (check with your county agricultural agent) or mechanically by removal of the surplus fruit in June. Before actually picking off any of the fruits, the branches should be shaken to dislodge any insecurely attached ones and any that are infested with insects. Enough apples and pears should be removed so that those remaining are spaced 6 or 8 inches apart, peaches 4 to 7 inches, plums 3 to 4. Among the benefits conferred by thinning the fruit are the following: the danger of breakage of branches due to the weight of fruit is lessened; it may help to prevent the tendency to become an alternate bearer; in the case of the stone fruits, the proportion of flesh to the inedible pit is higher; it helps to decrease brown-rot disease by promoting better air circulation; it makes it easier to achieve better coverage with pesticidal sprays or dust.

Pear (Beurre d'Anjou) trained to multiple U form on horizontal wires.

If you are interested in taking prizes for Grapes at the County Fair, thinning the number of berries in the bunch is desirable. Scissors with rounded points are used. Usually thinning is spread over a period of several weeks, starting when the Grapes are about the size of small peas, the idea being to leave each Grape ample room to grow without being crowded by its nearest neighbor.

The four-armed horizontal cordon method of espaliered Pear (Duchess d'Angoulême).

This shows how the Palmette Verrier system can be used to cover a solid south wall, 8 feet high, with Pear and Apple.

Espaliered figs at Williamsburg, Virginia, trained on a wood lattice.

This Apple trained in goblet shape was included in a *jardin potager* installed at the Chelsea Show, London, for the famous firm Vilmorin-Andrieux of Paris. It is estimated to be about forty years old. The growing and training of so complicated a specimen obviously is not an overnight job. It is one that requires skill and pertinacity. Starting with a one-year-old whip, it is cut back to about a foot above the surface of the soil. If growth is such that there are enough branches to make the first tier of shoots, the form or part of it can be installed now. Twelve stakes are placed equidistant around a hoop about 4 feet in diameter. At the beginning of the second year the growth made the preceding year probably warrants cutting the shoots to leave one or two growth buds on each. These as they grow should be trained almost horizontally toward the stakes, where they are tied. All laterals produced should be cut back to two or three buds. This is a continual chore and one that requires attention throughout the growing season. The object is to develop plenty of spurs about a foot apart. Also, the main branches must be watched and measures taken to keep them growing uniformly. Another requirement is to make the Y's, starting them at a height of about 5 or 6 feet, by cutting off the tips of the twelve main branches. Here again it is necessary to have a framework of bamboo or other stakes on which to train the stems. Most of this work must be done during the growing season. When the limit is reached the stems are trained in a circle. Sometimes it may be necessary to graft a flowering spur in a place where there is a gap on the stems. You must be really dedicated to the cult of training plants to attempt one so elaborate as this. In any case, you probably would do better to start with a single or double cordon or a Palmette Verrier.

CHAPTER XV

Kitchen Garden and Herbs

Pruning in the Kitchen Garden

Not much pruning needs to be done in the kitchen garden unless you look on thinning such crops as Carrots, Kohlrabi, Lettuce, etc., as forms of pruning. The one crop that really does need pruning is the Tomato when it is grown as a one- or two-stem plant. The advantage of this way of training Tomatoes is that it reduces the loss which seems to be inevitable when the bushes are unpruned so that the fruits develop in contact with the soil. One way of growing Tomatoes is to plant them about 18 inches apart in the row, 3 feet between the rows, with a stake near each plant. As the shoots increase in length each shoot should be tied to a stake. The axillary shoots which develop should be rubbed out before they get too large. When the original stem approaches a height of 3 feet, it is desirable to allow another stem to start from near the base. This will insure Tomatoes being produced until the plants are killed by frost. That is how it is done theoretically, but, if you are like me, by the time the plants are about 3 feet high you will find yourself swamped by the exuberant growth and give up the struggle to keep the axillary shoots picked off.

Herbs

It may seem like a contradiction in terms to include shrubs in an herb garden, but many herbs grown for fragrance or for culinary or medicinal purposes are woody plants and therefore are dealt with here.

One of the best ways to display herbs and at the same time put a little "oomph" in the herb garden is to do as they did in

Illustrating the correct method of tying a Tomato shoot—tightly on the stake, loosely on the plant.

Elizabethan times—make "knot gardens," which were greatly in favor then. The herbs that form the "thrids" of the knot must be naturally compact and/or kinds that can be kept so by pruning.

Among the best of the comparatively hardy kinds are: *Artemisia pontica* (Roman Wormwood), *Lavandula officinalis* (Lavender), especially such compact forms as Hidcote and Nana, *Teucrium chamaedrys* (Germander), *Ruta graveolens* (Rue), *Allium schoenoprasum* (Chive), and *Viola odorata* (Sweet Violet). Where mild winters are the rule, such as in Washington D.C., and southward, *Rosmarinus officinalis* (Rosemary), *Buxus sempervirens suffruticosa* (Dwarf Boxwood), *Santolina chamaecyparissus (incana)* (Lavender Cotton), and *S. virens* may be used. These can be added to those previously mentioned or substituted for the Sweet Violet and the Chive, thus making an all-shrubby knot.

Clean-cut lines are necessary for an effective knot. This involves frequent pruning, which can be done with grass or hedge shears. A spade is necessary to curb the Germander. This is operated by pushing the blade into the ground alongside the row to cut the underground spreading stems and then bearing down on the handle to throw out the superfluous parts, thus preventing it from becoming too "roynish and cumbersome." The portions cut off can be used for propagating.

An axillary shoot which should be pinched out. This is on a second shoot coming up from the base of the plant which will take over for the first shoot when production starts to decline.

Trimming Germander with grass shears.

Knot garden furnished with herbs in the Brooklyn Botanic Garden. Frequent pruning is necessary to keep the various members in bounds.

A knot garden from *The Gardeners Labyrinth,* by Dydymus Mountaine (Thomas Hill), 1571.

1. Thyme or Roman Wormwood
2. Sweet Violet or *Santolina virens*
3. Lavender Cotton or Dwarf Lavender
4. Germander or Rosemary

CHAPTER XVI

Insect Pests and Diseases

PRUNING is a valuable adjunct for the control of some insect pests, especially when it is done with timeliness.

Scale insects can be fought by cutting off the branches which are infested and destroying them by burning. This, usually, is only partly effective unless the trouble is diagnosed before the insects have a chance to really dig in. It is helpful to cut out the worst-infested branches when the insects are dormant during the winter.

See page 46 for removing black aphids from *Euonymus alatus compactus*.

Fire Blight, a bacterial disease of Pear, Apple and related trees and shrubs, can be fought in two ways by pruning. First, by avoiding severe pruning, which may cause the development of succulent shoots, called water sprouts, which are especially susceptible to the disease. Second, by cutting out affected branches,

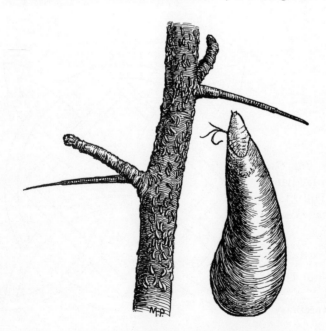

Oyster-Shell Scale.

Fire Blight on Quince. Dotted
line shows where to cut off infected branch.

making the cut at least a foot below the affected area. The pruning
tool should be disinfected after each cut by dipping it in Formalin
or alcohol and the prunings destroyed by burning.

Botrytis Blight, Phytophthora, Stem Rot, Leaf Blotch, and
Stem Spot are fungus diseases of Peony. All of these can be controlled by pruning out the affected parts of plants and by cutting
off the tops just below the surface of the ground in the fall and
destroying them by burning.

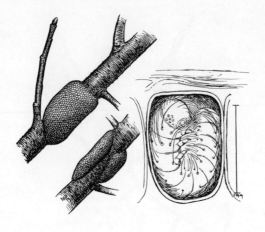

Tent Caterpillar egg masses.

It is possible to reduce materially the number of Tent Caterpillars by cutting off the twigs on which the egg masses of these loathsome insects are laid. The egg masses may contain from 150 to 300 eggs. They are dark brown in color, shiny, and laid in a belt around a twig. Cynthia Westcott says in *The Gardener's Bug Book* that it may be a good plan to gather the masses and put them in a cage of mosquito netting and leave them in the open so that the parasites, of which there are many affecting this species, may have an opportunity to emerge.

Blue-Spruce Gall Aphids make galls at the tips of young shoots of Colorado Blue, Engelman, Sitka, and Oriental Spruces. The galls should be cut off in June or early in July, before they open. This shows an open gall; insects have already emerged.

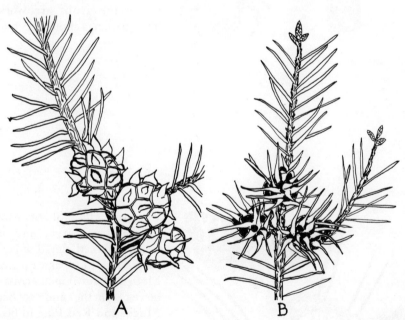

A   B

Eastern-Spruce Gall Aphid is responsible for the production of the pineapple-like galls which are found at the base of the shoots on Norway and White Spruces. Because of the location of the galls, cutting them off removes too much of the plant except when there are only a few present. A, closed gall. B, open gall; insects have emerged.

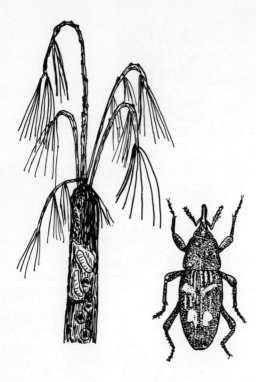

The White-Pine Weevil is a serious pest in the East. Its presence is shown by the browning of needles on terminal shoots. One remedy is pruning by cutting the dead shoots below the place where the grubs are working. The prunings should be burned.

European Pine-Shoot Moth—crooked tip, larva, and adult much enlarged, detail of larva in shoot. The European Pine-Shoot Moth is about ¾ inch across. The larva causes the candles of Scotch, Mugo, and Red Pine to become crooked and straw-colored. The infested candles should be broken off before the moth emerges in June or July, being sure to get the little caterpillar or pupa. These should be burned at once.

Index

ACKNOWLEDGMENTS

The following list shows the sources for photographs in this book. References are made to pages and the position of the respective photograph: t. top, b. bottom, c. center, r. right, l. left.

Bartlett Manufacturing Co.: 17 2nd. from t., 18 l., 19 b., 22 t.

Bartlett Tree Expert Co.: 256.

Beale, J. H.: 246 b.

Brooklyn Botanic Garden: 28, 34, 51 t., 56, 57, 73, 114, 190, 196, 202, 267, 269 t.

Buhle, Louis: 54, 55, 79 b., 83 b., 176 t.

Chanler, Mrs.: 141 b., 157 b., 158.

Cohen, Doris Darlington: 12, 13, 24 t. (2), 70, 83 t., 85, 96, 124, 181, 182 t., 189 b., 193, 198, 201 b., 207, 212, 242, 243, 258.

Corliss Brothers: 40, 144.

Costain, Harold Haliday: 261, 262, 263.

Free, Montague: 16 l., 17 t., b., 19 t., 23 t., c., 24 3rd. from t., b., 26, 27, 30, 31, 35, 36, 37, 39, 41, 43, 45, 48, 49, 50, 51 b., 52, 53, 59, 60, 61, 68, 69 t., 75, 76, 82, 84, 86, 88, 89, 90, 91 b. (2), 92, 93, 95 b., 100, 101, 103 b., 104, 105, 106, 108 b., 109, 113, 116, 117, 118, 119, 126, 127, 131, 132, 133, 134, 136, 138, 139 b., 141 t., 143, 145, 146 t., 147, 150, 154, 156, 157 t., 159, 160, 161, 162, 163, 166, 168, 169, 170, 171, 174, 176 b., 177, 178, 179, 180, 184 t., 186, 187, 189 t., 191, 192, 194, 197, 199, 200, 201 t., 205, 209, 210, 211, 213, 214, 216 b., 218, 219, 220 b., 225, 229, 230, 232, 233, 238, 246 t., 247, 248, 249 b., 250, 251, 252, 264, 268, 272 b.

Longwood Gardens, photo by G. Hampfler: 260.

Manigault, Edward L.: 149, 152.

Massachusetts Horticultural Society: 47.

McFarland, J. Horace: 151 t.

Melady, Eva: 64, 65, 66, 67.

Purdy, Maud H.: 24 4th. from t., 71, 72, 74, 77, 137, 151 b., 175, 206, 215, 231, 253, 259, 269 b., 270, 272 t.

Rebhan, J.: 112.

Rockwell, F. F.: 63, 69 b., 87.

Smith, Richard Averill: 95 t., 97, 98, 99, 115, 121, 128 b., 130 t., c., 226 l.

Steenson & Baker: 16 r., 20, 22 b., 23 b., 44, 107, 108 t., 120, 123, 128 t., 129, 135, 139 t., 164, 165, 172, 173, 182 b., 183 b., 184 b., 185, 188, 244.